THE STORY OF THE PEACE CORPS

THE STORY OF
THE PEACE CORPS

By George Sullivan

FLEET PUBLISHING CORPORATION

230 PARK AVENUE, NEW YORK

For permission to quote from their publications, the author makes grateful acknowledgment to the following:

For the quotation on Page 124, *The New Republic*, November 6, 1961, "A Question of Black or White," Copyright, 1961; for the quotation on Page 21, "Washington Merry-Go-Round," by Drew Pearson, "Peace Corps, 1918," Copyright, 1961, by Bell Syndicate, Inc.; for the quotation on Page 19, *Foreign Affairs*, July 1963, "Two Years of the Peace Corps," by Sargent Shriver, Page 694, Copyright 1961, *Foreign Affairs;* Page 100, *The Indianapolis Times*, July 19, 1963; Page 112, *Grit*, Williamsport, Penna., April 21, 1963; Page 116, *Pittsburgh Post Gazette and Sun Telegraph*, October 16, 1963; Page 98, *Providence (R.I.) Bulletin*, June 10, 1963; Page 115, *Waukesha (Wisc.) Freeman*, June 1, 1963; Page 112, *Denver Rocky Mountain News*, June 30, 1963; Page 141, *Seattle Post Intelligencer*, April 14, 1963.

THE STORY OF THE PEACE CORPS

For Midge

ACKNOWLEDGMENTS

The author wishes to acknowledge, with gratitude, the kind assistance of the following sources of information:

—Maurice L. Albertson, Director, Colorado State University Research Foundation
—Reed Alvord, Experiment in International Living
—Dr. Lawrence Fuchs, Dean of Faculty, Brandeis University
—Samuel P. Hayes, President, Foreign Policy Association of the United States
—Senator Hubert Humphrey
—Dr. Sidney M. Jourard, University of Florida
—Sam Kaufman, CARE, Inc.
—Max F. Millikan, Director, Massachusetts Institute of Technology, Center for International Studies
—Representative Henry S. Reuss
—Heinz Rollman
—Pierre Salinger
And these representatives of the Peace Corps for their cooperation:
—Robert Calvert, Jr., Director Peace Corps Volunteer Career Information Service
—Kenneth Coffee, Specialized Recruiting
—Dr. William Craig, Director of Training

—Dr. Leonard Duhl, Psychiatrist, Professional Services Branch, National Institute of Mental Health

—Dr. Joseph English, Chief Psychiatric Consultant

—Frank W. Erwin, Director of Operations, Division of Recruiting

—Robert Gale, Director of Recruiting

—Philip Hardberger, Division of Public Affairs

—James T. Walls, Public Information Officer

—Warren Wiggins, Director, Program Development and Operation

—Lloyd Wright, Deputy Associate Director

Contents

Introduction
BY SARGENT SHRIVER

On March 1, 1964, the third birthday of the Peace Corps,
we could add up he 7,500 Volunteers who, on that date,
were serving with distinction in 46 countries around the
world. We could insist, without sentimentality, that these
American men and women are the best, unofficial ambassadors that the United States has ever sent abroad, that
they are doing work that desperately needs doing, that the
sympathy and enthusiasm with which they have gone about
their tasks have made them as popular with the common
people of other nations as they are with the foreign governments who now ask us for two, three, even five and six
times as many Volunteers as we have already sent them.

On a birthday, however, the mind tends to drift back to
the days when it all began. I vividly recall that on March 1,
1961, when the Peace Corps was brought into existence by
executive order of President Kennedy, I had no idea—and

[xi

neither did anyone else—what kind of people the Volunteers would turn out to be.

In those days, there were plenty of people anxious to tell us that we were courting disaster in our eagerness to export platoons of Andy Hardys and their pony-tailed girl friends to the long-suffering underdeveloped nations of the world. We were also informed that luxury-loving Americans were too soft to live without electricity and hot and cold running water. We were asked what we expected to gain by sending innocents into areas where experts were having tough times. We were told that no one would volunteer for the Peace Corps except creeps, beatniks, visionaries, radicals and perpetual adolescents. It is obvious in retrospect that the people who said these things didn't know what they were talking about. Still, they talked often and loud enough to cause us a few qualms. Most of us involved in the Peace Corps's early days had more faith in the qualities and qualifications of Americans than the vociferous critics. I certainly did, or I would never have agreed to serve as Director of the Corps. Prospect, however, is a lot less certain than retrospect, and in those days, no one had seen a Volunteer because there weren't any yet.

With the help of a number of distinguished and brilliant people, I worked all through the month of February, 1961, getting the Peace Corps organized on paper. When President Kennedy called the Peace Corps into existence, we were ready to go. Among the various departments and divisions which, we had decided, were essential to operating a Peace Corps, was the Selection Division. This division was headed in those earliest days by an eminent psychologist and expert on selection procedures, Dr. Nicholas Hobbs, who has since returned to his regular job as Chairman of the Division of Human Development at George Peabody College for Teachers in Nashville, Tennessee. Dr. Hobbs didn't know exactly what the Volunteers were going to be like, either, but he knew more than the rest of us because he was charged with setting up the standards on the basis of which we would do our selecting. Very soon after our birthday (March 1, 1961), I too, took off on an extended tour—to Ghana, Nigeria, India, Pakistan, Burma, Malaya, Thailand and the Philippines—to inform the governments of these nations that the Peace Corps was now in business and to get an idea from them what sort of jobs they wanted Volunteers to do. While I was away, Nick Hobbs wrestled with his selection standards, honed them into shape and started applying them to the torrent of applications that flooded us during the weeks following opening day. When I returned from my trip, we still didn't know what the Volunteers were going to be like, but invitations had been sent out to those we considered our most acceptable applicants. We had signed a contract with Rutgers University to conduct our very first training program.

On June 25, 1961, slightly more than 60 men, most of them young, showed up at Rutgers to take training for a program of rural community development in the Latin American nation of Colombia. Here at last were our first Volunteers! For five months we had been talking about them, arguing over them, worrying about them and defending them, hypothetically, in the press, and here they were at last in the flesh. Now we would finally see what they were like. I had a final moment of trepidation on my way to Rutgers where I was scheduled to greet them in the name of the Peace Corps—could the critics be right, after all? When I finally stood in front of them to make a few remarks, I noticed that they were at least a fine looking group. When I had finished, I asked them if they had any questions—if they did, I would try to answer them. Instantly, their faces, passively listening until then, were transformed. They plunged into the question session with a kind of keyed-up enthusiasm and rock-hard intelligence. Soon we were laughing together when it became obvious that a lot of their questions couldn't be answered then, not until at least some Volunteers had gone overseas, and that then they would be better equipped to answer them than I. This was not a representative group of Volunteers since there were no women present. But it was a thrill for me, one that I will never forget, to see what kind of people we had attracted into the Peace Corps. I knew then that I could go back to Washington and tell the rest of the staff when they asked me what the Volunteers were like—and I did tell them—"Don't worry about the Volunteers. They're marvelous."

CHAPTER 1

The
History

IT was Wednesday, November 2, 1960. With election day less than a week away, the presidential campaigns were in their final, frenetic stages. For the first time, the smiling, confident figure of President Eisenhower stood by Richard Nixon's side, as the Republican standard-bearer launched a last ditch effort to capture New York's 45 electoral votes. Through a tumultuous day—uncommonly mild for November—they campaigned together through New York City, ending the saturation drive in a huge party rally at the New York Coliseum.

Candidate Kennedy, at the same time, sought to blitzkrieg the opposite coast. He was confident and buoyant now. His campaign machinery was purring smoothly and he was thriving on his 20-hour-a-day schedule. The weekly news magazines had just announced predictions of his victory. Huge, frenzied crowds, expressing the new-found charisma of the Kennedys, had greeted him earlier in the week in Los Angeles.

For Senator Kennedy, November 2 began with a break-fast rally at the Beverly Hilton Hotel in Los Angeles where he spoke to 1,700 women. Then, there was a quick trip south to San Diego before the candidate flew on to the Bay area of San Francisco. Here, there was a rally and quick speech in San Jose (where three police officers were injured in the crush), and then a brief address to thousands at Oakland's deFremery Park. At every stop, he was hailed by throngs of what one newspaper described as "screamers, runners, exhorters and jumpers."

Early that evening, more than 1,500 enthusiastic Democrats assembled at a $100-a-plate dinner at San Francisco's Sheraton Palace Hotel to hear their candidate chide Eisenhower's eleventh hour participation in the campaign as a "rescue mission." The most important event of the frantic day, a huge rally in the Cow Palace, San Francisco's anomalously-named cattle exhibition auditorium, was saved for last.

Two hours before the candidate arrived, 25,000 people jammed the hall to its capacity. Another 5,000 surged through the corridors outside the auditorium itself and they chanted, "We want in! We want in!" Their cries blended with those of the partisans inside the auditorium who, as they waited, cheered, "We want Kennedy! We want Kennedy!"

Then, just before the candidate arrived, the outsiders broke through a door from the corridor and spilled into the arena. No seats were available, so they stood in the aisles. When the smiling and assured Senator appeared, there was a near riot. The more than 25,000 supporters roared a tumultuous welcome; it was several minutes before they were quiet.

This was a major address, and the candidate reflected its importance with a quiet confidence. Speaking to his uproarious supporters, who punctuated his every sentence with screams and cheers, Candidate Kennedy called for the establishment of a pool of "talented young men willing to serve . . . in the under-developed world." He called for "Ambassadors of Peace," for skilled Americans who "could work, building goodwill, building the peace." That night, in the raging melee of the Cow Palace in San Francisco, the American Peace Corps was born.

Though the idea for a Peace Corps–type program had been adrift in political circles for almost a decade, Candidate Kennedy's speech to the wild throng in San Francisco brought the idea to life. Coming as it did, in the final stages of an intensely interesting and hard fought campaign for the presidency; coming as it did with the news media of the nation and the world sharply focused on the speaker, the idea of a "Peace Corps of young Americans" became the major news of the day. It was front-paged in a thousand daily newspapers. It was hailed on television and radio. Thirty thousand Americans wrote to support the idea (Press Secretary Salinger said no topic during the campaign received as much mail); thousands of these volunteered to join.

Director of the Peace Corps, Sargent Shriver, writing in *Foreign Affairs* magazine, observed that Oscar Wilde commented at one time that America really was discovered by a dozen people before Columbus, "but it was always successfully hushed up." Wrote Mr. Shriver: "I am tempted to feel that way about the Peace Corps; the idea of a national effort of this type had been proposed many times in past years." Indeed, it had.

"Volunteer assistance," of the brand offered by the Peace Corps, was apparent very early in our country's history. Since 1809, churches of the United States have been sending missionaries abroad. And the missionaries perform many tasks besides preaching the gospel. They teach school; they teach trades. They build hospitals and educate doctors and nurses. They develop health and social welfare programs; they help the farmers. This is much the nature of the Peace Corps work.

Today, American missionaries and missionary agencies are a powerful force overseas. The statistics are impressive: the people of the United States, through 400 separate religious agencies, maintain 34,000 missionaries abroad— 27,000 Protestant and 7,000 Catholic. Jewish organizations contribute skilled technicians, doctors, and teachers.

Overseas assistance is also motivated outside of the religious sphere. American business organizations, philanthropic foundations, and non-religious volunteer agencies aid peoples and countries around the world medically, educationally, and technically. To be sure, this is not solely an American bent. Most every nation of the world has its groups of mission organizations and government supported and volunteer agencies which carry on programs for underprivileged people and under-developed nations. The structure of the United Nations is proliferated with a dozen agencies offering overseas people-to-people assistance of every kind.

One American agency that has long been on the forefront in providing people-to-people assistance in foreign countries is the American Friends Service Committee. As far back as 1919, this Quaker organization was at work. In that year, under American Friends sponsorship, a group of

young people sailed for the Balkans where they spent two
years repairing some of the chaos of World War I. Their
activity was much like latter-day Peace Corps volunteers;
they rebuilt farms, houses, and schools, and they established hospitals. Columnist Drew Pearson was a member of
the group and his comments on the adventure are typical of
those heard from returning Peace Corps volunteers of the
1960's. Says Mr. Pearson, "I realize that the two years I
contributed to selling peace in the Balkans did a lot more
for me than it did for the Balkans."

Twenty years before Mr. Pearson's sojourn, a more typical example of American Peace Corps–type of activity was
launched in the Philippines. In size and type, in philosophy
and in motivation, it was in many ways similar to our
present day Peace Corps teaching contingent in the archipelago. Called "Thomasites," after the converted battle
cruiser, "Thomas," that brought them to the islands, this
group of more than a thousand volunteer teachers taught
the young and ministered to the sick. Their work in the
Philippines between 1901 and 1933 was performed under
great handicap for they lacked official government sanction; they had no military protection and little in the way
of health facilities. During the first 20 months, 27 of them
died. Yet their decades of service helped to establish a bond
of loyalty and friendship between the Filipinos and Americans that was greatly apparent during the horrifying days
of World War II.

Following every major war, there is an effort on the part
of the altruistic and perhaps conscience-stricken victorious
nations to lend assistance to the dispirited people of defeated countries. So it was after the Spanish American War
as typified by the "Thomasites." So it was after World

War I. The work of the American Friends is an example. So it was after World War II. A great outpouring of American assistance was launched, completely unrivaled by any type of program that the world had ever known. Private agencies like CARE were established. Government agencies like UNRRA swung into action. The Marshall Plan was activated. The newly-formed United Nations supported assistance agencies to distribute food, to care for the sick, to educate. Dr. Samuel P. Hayes, President of the Foreign Policy Association, in a pamphlet titled, "An International Peace Corps," published in 1961, listed no less than 26 private organizations that were, at that time, carrying on volunteer service programs overseas. Of course, many programs—particularly government sponsored programs—are almost purely financial in the type of assistance they offer. They do not boast the "people-to-people" feature of the Peace Corps.

In 1948, in his inaugural address, President Harry Truman announced a new program "to help the free peoples of the world" to realize "their aspirations for a better life." This became known as the "Point Four Program" and was instituted to provide assistance for so-called "under-developed peoples." It was a program characteristic of the time. It evolved into the ICA (the International Cooperation Agency), and presently the AID (the Agency for International Development). Early in 1961, the ICA had 9,000 skilled technicians working in more than 70 nations overseas. When Senator Kennedy called for the establishment of the Peace Corps in his speech at the Cow Palace in November, 1960, he recommended that the new agency be "directed and paid by ICA–Point Four agencies." (But, instead, the Peace Corps was established as a wing of the State Department and given separate status.)

Against this American policy and even tradition of country-to-country relief and support, the Peace Corps idea developed. Yet it is difficult to say who first phrased the idea in its present terms.

Many sources, including the Peace Corps itself, trace the idea for such an organization back to the nineteenth century American philosopher and psychologist William James. He called for a "conscription of our youthful population" to form "an army against Nature." Once conscripted, the youths would be assigned "to coal and iron mines, to freight trains, to fishing fleets in December, to dishwashing, to clothes washing, and window washing, to road building and tunnel making, to foundries and stoke holes, and to frames of skyscrapers." Philosopher James' idea wasn't entirely altruistic. He felt that our population was grasped by a war function, that "pugnacity had been bred into our bone and marrow," and he felt assigning our youth into disciplined service would endow them with "healthier sympathies" and "soberer ideas." Their "war function," he said, would be supplanted. Mr. James' thoughts were related pretty much to the domestic sphere; he expressed no desire for his army to help indigent people of developing countries.

In the United States political arena, the idea for a Peace Corps–type organization was probably first propounded by a refugee from wartime Germany named Heinz Rollman. Now a Waynesville, North Carolina industrialist—a major shoe manufacturer—Rollman first visited the United States in the 1930's. Returning to his native Germany after a brief stay in this country, he proclaimed a "United States of

Europe" as the only alternative to a second world war. Plans on this grandiose a scale come naturally to Mr. Rollman. He is a quick, restless, energetic idea man.

Adolph Hitler seized Rollman's industrial plants and holdings in Germany and Belgium in the 1930's. In 1939, Mr. Rollman settled permanently in the United States and during the post World War II years took on an avid letter-writing campaign, directed to top government officials, suggesting that the way to win the peace was to solve the problems of the world's under-developed countries. "In that way, too," he said, "the onrush of world Communism could be halted."

Mr. Rollman proposed an all-embracing movement among the nations of the world, an idea he called "World Construction." Under its terms, the nations of the world would organize as actively and efficiently for peace as they did for war. His ideas were warmly received by Mrs. Eleanor Roosevelt, and at her suggestion, he set down his plan in book form. His book, titled *World Construction,* was published in 1954 by Greenberg Publishers of New York, and he made a wide distribution of his treatise among congressional leaders and government officials.

A portion of his idea for *World Construction* called for Congress to establish a vast "Peace Army" consisting of three million American men and women who would be sent to the world's under-privileged, under-developed countries. This army of technical teachers would seek to end the imbalances that existed between nations in farming, housing, industry, distribution, and communication.

Through the 1950's, Mr. Rollman carried out a personal promotion campaign to establish his Peace Army plan. He continued his letter-writing efforts, and he button-holed leading government officials. Twice he succeeded in getting his proposals before President Eisenhower, and twice he ran for Congress on a Peace Army platform. (He was defeated both times, but the last time, in 1960, he polled 48 per cent of the vote.) Though Mr. Rollman has been mentioned in Congress as the father of the Peace Corps idea, his activity was able to establish little of concrete value. He lacked a platform; he lacked popular support. He lacked the active and avowed interest of Congressional leaders.

Of more tangible value in establishing the Peace Corps was the work of Congressman Henry S. Reuss, a Wisconsin Democrat who represents the Milwaukee area of his state. Late in 1957, he propounded the idea of a "Youth Corps," to be formed under the aegis of the Point Four Program of the Mutual Security Act, and to provide service of the nature of the Peace Corps of today.

Congressman Reuss recalls that his idea for such a program came to him while conducting a foreign aid inspection tour in the fall of 1957 in the Far East. In the jungles of Cambodia, he came upon a group of four American school teachers who were going from village to village setting up elementary schools. He was awed by the respect, by the love, he says, that the native population had for the young Americans. The United States had built a thirty million dollar highway through the Cambodian jungle that received little use, and Congressman Reuss reflected on how many more benefits the United States was able to reap from the work of the dedicated teachers, than the country gained from the construction of the highway.

With the experience in Cambodia fresh in his mind, the Congressman made a formal expression to establish a Point Four Selective Service for young Americans, for those willing to serve their country "in far-off places at soldier's pay." His proposal was made in a speech at Cornell University in April, 1958, and according to Congressman Reuss, the response to the idea was "electric." He continued to refine and discuss and propose the idea, finding the response never less than enthusiastic.

In January, 1960, Congressman Reuss' interest in a "Youth Corps" resulted in legislation he introduced in the House—it was co-sponsored in the Senate by the late Senator Richard Neuberger of Oregon—calling for the appropriation of $10,000 to study the feasability of the Point Four "Youth Corps" idea. Passed as a rider to the Mutual Security Act, the bill became law in September, 1960. The ICA contracted the research study to the Colorado State University Research Foundation in Fort Collins. The report that evolved was as comprehensive as any report could be and served importantly in the development of Peace Corps programs and policies.

Congressman Reuss says that the idea of a "Youth Corps" for the nation is not particularly a unique one. He cites IVS (International Voluntary Services, Inc.), a coordinating agency for a group of 15 church denominations interested in private technical assistance programs, as carrying on activity similar to what he felt the "Youth Corps" should. Beginning in the early 1950's, IVS sent teams of young Americans to such countries as Laos, Viet Nam, and to Egypt, to train native citizens in agriculture, farm mechanics, animal husbandry, home economics, and the like. According to Congressman Reuss, their work met with great success.

Senator Hubert Humphrey of Minnesota was another Congressional leader in the front rank in the development and establishment of the Peace Corps. He first came upon the idea in action when he observed the work of the afore-mentioned American Friends Service Committee. Impressed with their work, he, too, proposed the idea to college groups during the late 1950's and he found his suggestions met with the same strong, enthusiastic response as had those of Congressman Reuss. However, at this time, he says, the idea was not taken seriously in official government circles. He assigned members of his staff—principally a Stanford University foreign relations researchist named Peter Grothe—to research the idea for him, and the results of these studies increased his fervor for the program.

In June, 1960, Senator Humphrey formally introduced legislation in the Senate calling for the establishment of a "Peace Corps," although Congress was scheduled for adjournment and action on the measure was considered unlikely. According to the Senator, he was "deluged with mail" in favor of the idea, and he was also heartened by the fact that there was little Congressional opposition to the legislation. There was some critical feeling toward the Senator's actions, however, for in some quarters it was felt his legislation could have been more appropriately introduced after the Colorado State University research report was completed. There was also concern that Senator Humphrey's proposal would duplicate or conflict with ICA efforts.

During the summer and into the fall of presidential election-year 1960, Peace Corps–type programs were being proposed on several fronts. Mr. Rollman was active in North Carolina. Bill Moyers, now Deputy Director of the Peace Corps, at that time supervised campaign activity for Vice-Presidential candidate Johnson, and prepared at least two

campaign speeches suggesting the Peace Corps idea. Chester
Bowles, Mr. Kennedy's foreign relations adviser during the
campaign, used the idea as speech material. Victor Reuther,
of the UAW propounded the idea. General James Gavin
had spoken of it.

Senator Kennedy first proposed the Peace Corps concept
at this time, too. On October 14, in an extemporaneous
speech at the University of Michigan delivered at 2 A.M.
before 9,000 students, he talked about the good that young
people might be able to do in overseas service, though he
didn't use the phrase "Peace Corps." While his talk did not
attract much nationwide attention—the campaign press
plane had leapfrogged ahead—a wild student response
greeted his remarks and he was impressed.

Two weeks later, in San Francisco, the major speech on
the Peace Corps was delivered. Much of the material that
was included in the address was gathered by chief campaign
speech writer, and now Solicitor General, Archibald Cox,
while Ted Sorenson, a top Kennedy aide, and until February, 1964, Special Counsel to President Johnson, was the
principal author of the text. Senator Kennedy directed that
the Peace Corps issue be prepared as a major address, and
there are a good many reasons why he chose the time and
place that he did to endorse and expound the idea.

First, the idea, to use the words of Press Secretary Salinger, had been "gradually building," and San Francisco was
looked on as an appropriate forum to make a formal campaign endorsement of the program. Such an announcement, some campaign advisers felt, would be helpful in
winning the votes of Stevensonian Democrats and liberal
Republicans. Second, there was a rumor (later found to
be untrue) that Nixon forces were planning to make an

announcement of *their* endorsement of a Peace Corps or a Youth Corps. Third, other campaign issues had worn thin; by now, they created little interest. Finally, the candidate knew, on the basis of the idea's reception at the University of Michigan, that the Peace Corps would be a popular issue with the people. (It was. In a Gallup poll, 71 per cent of Americans backed the Corps idea; 66 per cent wanted their sons to join it.)

Senator Kennedy's speech enlarged upon the proposals of Reuss and Senator Humphrey and the others. It opened the Peace Corps to women; it softened the age requirements—it was not to be just a "Youth Corps." The speech to the candidate's later consternation, suggested that Peace Corps service could be an "alternative to peace-time selective service." Though never adopted as part of the Peace Corps program, this suggestion brought sharp criticism from the Republican side. GOP candidates, Vice-President Nixon among them, declared the Peace Corps "to be a haven for draft dodgers."

Senator Kennedy's speech touched off a great wave of enthusiasm for the Peace Corps. Letters and telegrams poured into Washington. On college campuses throughout the country, study groups and clubs were organized on behalf of the idea. It was not because the idea was particularly new; the speech did, however, to quote Dr. Samuel Hayes, now head of the Foreign Policy Association, Inc. and an early Peace Corps adviser, lift the idea "to a much higher level and to a much broader scope. . . ." John F. Kennedy had the courage and the vision to make the Peace Corps national policy.

Shortly after taking office in January, 1961, President Kennedy set up a study committee—the newspapers called it a "task force"—under Sargent Shriver, calling him from his job as President of the Chicago Board of Education, to develop and round out the Peace Corps idea and to prepare a comprehensive report for him. The work was to be completed by March 1. Late in January, Mr. Shriver set up temporary headquarters in a two-room suite in Washington's Mayflower Hotel and began to arrange meetings and conferences with specialists from business, from government agencies, and from private and volunteer organizations. Some of those he called upon included:

—Warren Wiggins, now Peace Corps Director for Program Development and Operations, came to the Peace Corps in response to a 3 A.M. telegram from Sargent Shriver. Deputy Director of the ICA and a veteran of 12-years experience with United States aid programs abroad, Mr. Wiggins had prepared a paper entitled, "The Towering Task," based on his two and one half years ICA experience in the Philippines, and it came to be considered one of the clearest expositions of the Peace Corps idea.

—Dr. Max F. Millikan, Director of the Center for International Studies, Massachusetts Institute of Technology, contributed a 22-page memorandum concerning an "International Youth Service." (The memo was prepared in December, 1960, at the request of Chester Bowles who was asked by President-elect Kennedy to collect views on the Peace Corps idea.) The memorandum contained clear-cut statements as to the need for skilled people in underdeveloped countries, and made recommendations as to how young people could fill the demand. The principles set forth in this memorandum are—that the Peace Corps should be a semi-autonomous agency; that the standards of selection should be maintained at a high level; that volunteers should serve in an operational (not advisory) capacity—came to be Peace Corps policy. Presidential adviser Walter Rostow and Carroll Wilson, also of MIT, were contributors to Dr. Millikan's memo.

—Dr. Samuel P. Hayes, now President of the Foreign Policy Association, Inc., a private organization engaged in general citizen education on world affairs, prepared a memorandum in September, 1960, at the request of presidential adviser Archibald Cox, that outlined an idea for "An International Youth Service." With extensive experience in international economic programs, Dr. Hayes' report was one of the first to enunciate the "middle manpower" theme. Unskilled labor in under-developed countries is usually plentiful, the report said, and "top leadership can be found." But, said the report, "a gap exists in the middle levels." The memo pointed up in low income countries, shortages of personnel that existed with college, university, and professional training, with teaching, craft, art, farming, and organizing skills. It is these "shortages" the Peace Corps seeks to fill today.

—Dr. F. Gordon Boyce, Director, The Experiment in International Living (a private, non-profit educational organization that arranges for interested Americans, particularly American youth, the "experience" of living with a family in another country), was named Director of the Division of Private Organizations. (Sargent Shriver had been an "Experimenter" to Germany and Austria in 1934 and 1936, and he served as a "Leader" to a group assigned to France in 1939. Congressman Reuss' wife and son were also "Experimenters.") Many staff members of the Experiment in International Living were drawn to the Peace

Corps. Dr. Boyce and the organization, in providing both advice and training facilities, have played an important part in the organization and development of the Peace Corps.

Others who contributed to the formation of basic policies during the first days of Peace Corps activity were Albert G. Sims, Executive Vice President of the Institute of International Education; Carl Bode, now with AID; Harris Wofford, Peace Corps Representative for Africa; Richard Goodwin, Deputy Assistant Secretary of State; William Josephson, Peace Corps General Counsel; and James Grant, Assistant Secretary of State for the Near East. Of course, Senator Humphrey and Congressman Reuss attended meetings to lend their support and impart their advice and experience.

Peace Corps headquarters were moved from the Mayflower Hotel to the sixth floor of the Maiatico Building on Connecticut Avenue (where the Peace Corps is located today), and into these offices streamed counselors representing a wide range of interests: from university presidents and professors and labor leaders to mountain climbers and veterans of African safaris.

In February, Dr. Maurice Albertson, Director of Colorado State University's Research Foundation, submitted a preliminary report to Sargent Shriver's task force on the Point Four Youth Corps study as authorized by Congress. With two associates, he had visited Nigeria and Gabon, in Africa; Thailand, India, Pakistan, and the Philippines, in Asia; Colombia, Mexico, Chile, and Haiti, in Latin America. (With the exception of Mexico and Haiti, all are Peace Corps "host" countries today.) The team found projects that could use up to 5,000 volunteers.

The report was an all-embracing one. It set objectives for the Peace Corps to follow and recommended an organizational structure. It proposed selection and training methods for volunteers and for supervisory personnel. It stated terms and conditions of Peace Corps service. It suggested areas in which volunteers would be most successful: education, community development, and health and sanitation. Except for its recommendation that the Peace Corps should eventually become a part of the Agency for International Development (AID), major policies, and minor recommendations, too, set forth in the report were fairly well followed by Peace Corps administrators.

Generally, the Colorado State University study group was enthusiastic about the prospects of the Peace Corps. In part, their enthusiasm was engendered by their observation of Britain's Voluntary Service Organization, begun in 1959 as a "middleman agency," to recruit British youths for service in under-developed countries. With the help of British churchmen and the government, the VSO was launched by Alec Dickson, a UNESCO social worker and, at the time the agency was observed by the Colorado State University study group, the VSO had 200 volunteers working with "astonishing success" in 25 countries.

Late in February, Sargent Shriver, drawing from all of these diverse sources, completed his report for the White House. And on March 1, 1961, President Kennedy issued an Executive Order that established the Peace Corps on a "temporary pilot basis." It recommended that a "minimum of several hundred volunteers" be selected, trained, and at work before the end of the year. Funds for the new agency were to be provided out of the Mutual Security Act foreign aid program.

The order stressed that, at this stage, at least, the Peace Corps was to be purely "experimental in nature." But it recommended to Congress "the establishment of a permanent Peace Corps." Though it sought only to get the Peace Corps started, the Executive Order did rankle some congressmen who felt, as in the case of almost any Executive Order, that their legislative power was being usurped.

It was in this period that the problems and the criticism of the Peace Corps began to mount. First of all, there was no guarantee that Congress would sanction the Peace Corps idea. And even if they did approve the program, there was doubt that Congress would grant enough money to make the plan worthwhile. "Let Shriver live with his Executive Order for a year," said one legislator.

The name "Peace Corps" came in for criticism. To some the word "peace" was suspect because, in the sphere of government-sponsored propaganda, at least, the word was held to be the exclusive property of the Communists: the word "corps" was feared because of its military connotations. Dozens of alternative names were suggested. But "Peace Corps" was decided upon, for it was felt that the general conduct of the agency and its programs would give the name its character.

Fears were expressed that the Peace Corps was too strongly youth-oriented. The agency was dubbed "a second children's crusade," and "Kennedy's Kiddie Korps." However, Sargent Shriver felt the youthful enthusiasm of the organization was a great asset, though he felt—as did Senator Humphrey—that it had to be tempered with adult-minded pragmatism and with supervision.

Some congressional legislators felt the Peace Corps should not be government affiliated. There was a mild feeling that the agency would only supplant services that were already being carried on by experienced agencies outside government service.

Perhaps the hottest controversy revolved around the Peace Corps' intention of signing administrative contracts with American religious organizations to cover specific and individual overseas programs. Under this program, the church related agency was to agree to sign an anti-proselytizing pledge. With the announcement of this, a sharp church-state controversy flared up. Late in 1961, the whole policy of religious tie-ins was abandoned.

After the signing of the Executive Order, Sargent Shriver and his growing staff moved quickly to set up a functioning organization. Veteran Washington observers said that not since WPA depression days had a new government agency gone into action so fast. There were many problems. There was doubt that there were enough talented and qualified Americans willing to respond to the invitation to serve. And, if there were enough, could the right ones be selected? How were the recruits to be trained? How would the presence of Peace Corps volunteers react upon foreign service representatives overseas? Were Americans physically equipped to serve in isolated areas under primitive conditions? Could volunteers deal with anti-American sentiment? Could they cope with Communist agitation?

Out of the work sessions that were set up to solve these problems and others like them, two pieces of overriding policy were developed that came to serve as the backbone for the entire structure of the Peace Corps. First, it was decided that volunteers were to be "doers," not advisers. They were to work under a host country supervisor and in cooperation with host country co-workers, but no matter how they were to be directed, they were to perform, to move, to be in action.

(Equally important was the policy that dictated Peace Corps units would go only where invited. Volunteers are never foisted upon foreign countries. Volunteers fill a need, but more importantly, their overseas assignment complies with a formal request.

(In May, 1961, Sargent Shriver made a month-long survey tour of Africa and Asia in an effort to determine overseas interest in the new agency. With Harris Wofford, Edwin Bayley, former Executive Assistant to the Governor of Wisconsin and, later, Director of Public Information for the Peace Corps, and Franklin Williams, a former NAACP official, Mr. Shriver met with government officials in eight countries. He was pleased with the results of the trip. India wanted agricultural volunteers; Ghana needed teachers and electricians; the Philippines asked for English teachers. Following Mr. Shriver's return, estimates for the number of volunteers needed for the 1961 pilot program were revised upward. Instead of the original 300 to 500, plans for 1,000 were prepared.

On June 14, 1961, the first 12 volunteers were selected for service. And by the end of the year, 700 were on overseas assignment or in training in the United States.

On September 22, the same year, the Peace Corps, by virtue of the "Peace Corps Act" became law. The purposes and policies of the agency were made official; money was granted for its activity.

Congress established a "Declaration of Purpose" for the Peace Corps. This "mandate," as Peace Corps officials call it, set three basic objectives for the agency: first, the Peace Corps was to provide "interested countries" volunteers "qualified" for service abroad and willing to serve "under conditions of hardship if necessary" to help the people of these nations meet their needs for trained manpower. Second, the Peace Corps was to help "promote a better understanding of the American people on the part of the people served. . . ." And, third, the Peace Corps was to help provide a "better understanding of other peoples on the part of the American people.")

If the Peace Corps' activity is to be judged on the basis of this mandate, then the agency has been an immense success. In line with the Congressional recommendations, the Peace Corps has sent "qualified" volunteers to "interested countries"; it has promoted a better understanding of the American people on the part of the people served, and vice versa. By its very nature, the Peace Corps has accomplished these objectives. Asked to name the single outstanding accomplishment of the Peace Corps, Sargent Shriver states, "We have done what we have been told to do." The agency has, indeed.

The future of the Peace Corps is bright. Congress has always held the Peace Corps in the highest esteem and has demonstrated a continuing policy of treating Peace Corps budget requests with favor. At no time has there been serious congressional resistance to Peace Corps policies.

From the beginning, President Johnson has had a warm interest in Peace Corps activity. He was Chairman of the organization's National Advisory Committee, which is a group of private citizens representing religious, labor, and service organizations, established to advise about Peace Corps policy. As Vice-President, Mr. Johnson received weekly advisory reports on Peace Corps operations and, according to one official, "He read them."

The nation's interest in the Peace Corps remains high. According to Peace Corps selection officials, more than 50,-000 applications for service are expected to be received during 1964, more than double the amount received the previous year.

In assessing any area of Peace Corps activity, or in evaluating the agency as a whole, it is the volunteer and the work of the volunteer that must be appraised. Success or failure of the Peace Corps—the future of the organization— is in the hands of its overseas personnel. If the volunteers' spirit of dedication and feeling of responsibility can be maintained, and if their performance record can be kept at the current high levels, then the future of the Peace Corps will be illustrious, indeed.

CHAPTER 2

The
Membership

IT is a tribute, either to the American public generally, particularly to its youth, or to the public affairs and recruitment personnel of the Peace Corps, that application figures continue to run at such lofty heights. Doubtlessly, both groups share credit. For stripped of its sometimes glamor and its sundry human value appeals, little is offered by Peace Corps service. Succinctly, a recruit agrees to two years of rugged duty in a foreign country; and for that he is proffered wages that hardly approach the legal minimum.

In brief, the Peace Corps seeks men or women, single or married, age 18 or over. All tours of duty are for two years; there are no exceptions. Volunteers get 10 days vacation period following their training. They get free medical care; they get free transportation.

They receive $75 a month in what is termed a "readjustment allowance." It accrues for them while they are in service and is paid to the volunteer upon separation. Sargent Shriver recalls at the time Peace Corps policies were

being formulated in March, 1961, he decided that Peace
Corps volunteers should be the lowest paid workers in the
Federal establishment. And, in 1961, army privates, paid
$85 a month, were the smallest salaried government work-
ers. In addition to their readjustment allowance, volunteers are granted modest food, clothing, and housing ex-
pense reimbursements.

Volunteers receive 45 days leave for each 21 months
overseas. They are not allowed to use this leave-time to
return to the United States, but, instead, they are encouraged to tour in the country in which they are working.
Occasionally, they are allowed and even encouraged to
travel to countries adjacent to or nearby their host country.

Volunteers are not tax exempt, and their readjustment
allowance and some of their maintenance expenses are subject to federal income tax. And, in some cases, volunteer's
emoluments are subject to home-state taxation, too. All
volunteers are covered by Social Security and, if they want,
by $10,000 term life insurance. But payments in connec-
tion to both of these are deducted from their readjustment payment.

Since Peace Corps service has been classified as being
"within the national interest," volunteer draft selection is
always deferred until the term of service is completed. This
stricture subdued early critics of the Peace Corps who
tabbed the organization as a future haven for draft dodgers.

Despite the rather meager material rewards, the Peace
Corps membership has shown consistent growth—as most
everyone hoped it would. In the early months of 1961,
most officials of the Peace Corps estimated that 300 to
500 volunteers would provide a worthwhile pilot program.
But, following Sargent Shriver's eight-nation survey tour
through Africa and Asia in May 1961, the estimates were

revised upward. There were about 1,000 volunteers in the initial stages of the program. Today, there are roughly ten times that number.

By September 1, 1962, volunteer strength was put at 2,781. A year later, it had increased to 6,614, although 9,000 had been estimated for that date. Explains Director Shriver: "We have taken the advice not to grow so fast that we will sacrifice our efficiency." By August 31, 1964, 10,500 volunteers are expected to be in service.

By January 1, 1964, 600 volunteers had completed their two years of service, and during the course of 1964, an additional 3,000 volunteers were scheduled to be separated. About 10 per cent of those who have completed their service period request to extend their duty for periods ranging from three months to one year. One young lady, Hazel Land, of Miami, Florida, has been allowed to extend her period of service for an additional two years, though this practice is much more the exception than the rule. In fact, two-year enlistment extensions are generally frowned upon by top level Peace Corps officials.

Washington-based staff personnel, in September, 1962, made up close to 20 per cent of the total membership of the Peace Corps. But the following year, the number of staff personnel, on a proportionate basis, decreased significantly:—of the total membership of 9,000, about 10 per cent, 1,051 people, to be precise, were Washington staff. Peace Corps officials are sensitive about the charge the agency is fast becoming a monolithic government bureau. The Peace Corps is growing, but the proportion of Washington staffers is on the decline, as the figures above indicate. In this regard, the Peace Corps has a record other government agencies can envy.

Originally it was felt the Peace Corps membership

should be kept to around 10,000 men and women. However, during 1962, President Kennedy and Secretary of State Rusk requested Director Shriver to provide an additional 3,000 volunteers for Latin America, so membership rolls were revised upwards. There was a request for additional Africa-based volunteers, too.

Early in Peace Corps history, there were just about twice as many men volunteers as women. But the women are beginning to catch up. Early in 1964, they comprised 38 per cent of the total membership. Among men, the average age is 24.5 years; among women, 25.8 years—probably not as young as the public image of the Peace Corps volunteer would convey.

There are more than 400 married couples in Peace Corps service, including about 40 couples who met and married after joining. The Peace Corps welcomes "young marrieds"; it has found them extremely industrious.

Though it isn't often realized, the Peace Corps volunteers are not always just-out-of-college youngsters. Forty-two of them are between 50 and 60. Thirty-three are older than 60. The oldest is 77, a civil engineer from Texas whose name is Ralph Cole. He serves in Pakistan.

Also sprinkled through the volunteer membership are approximately 200 teenagers, boys and girls of 18 and 19. (Eighteen is the minimum age for volunteer service.) Teenagers as a group have a keen interest in the Peace Corps, particularly in volunteer service. In some high schools, Peace Corps Clubs are active among students. They keep in touch with overseas volunteers, help support volunteer work by supplying books and other educational essentials, and generally work to promote the Peace Corps concept in the high school and the community. One "youth" survey showed, that of the more than 1,200 youngsters interviewed, 53 per cent said they would like to join the Peace Corps.

Peace Corps youngsters are an exceptionally well educated group. Ninety per cent have completed a formal course of college study. Seventy-five per cent have bachelor's degrees, and eight per cent have master's degrees.

Dr. Nicholas Hobbs, the Peace Corps' first Director of Selection, says that, before applying for service, the average Peace Corps volunteer could boast an acquaintance with a foreign culture that far exceeded the ordinary. A substantial number, up to 25 per cent, studied or resided abroad for periods of more than four months. And most all volunteers have some degree of competence with a second language.

More than 1,500 colleges and universities are represented in the Peace Corps membership. The University of California ranks as the number one source of volunteers; Harvard is second.

The volunteer membership fairly well represents a cross section of the country's ethnic and religious strata, though officials agree that early interest on the part of Catholic youth was sluggish. The Catholic weekly, *America,* was "chilled" by the fact that, of the 62 volunteers serving in Catholic Colombia late in 1962, only two were graduates of Catholic colleges. Catholic participation in, and sponsorship of, lay missionary organizations may account for this seeming lack of interest. Lately, however, Catholic participation in the Peace Corps has become more proportionate to Catholic student body membership totals.

By region, the West Coast is well represented. California, alone, claims close to 15 per cent of the volunteer membership, to lead all other states. New York is second; Pennsyl-

vania, third; Illinois, fourth. Massachusetts, ninth ranked
in population, is fifth ranked in Peace Corps membership.
Proportionately, few volunteers come from Southern states.
(Dr. Hobbs explains that the South characteristically lags
in its tendency to supply candidates for Peace Corps–type
opportunities, and for fellowships, Fulbright appointments,
and research grants.)

The percentage of Negroes among the volunteers runs
considerably below 10 per cent—the percentage of Negroes
in the total United States population. The reasons advanced are mostly economic ones, though there is a feeling
that many Negroes feel their first duty is at home, helping
members of their own race.

The Peace Corps is organized into five major divisions:
Public Affairs, Program Development and Operations, The
Volunteers, Planning and Evaluation, and Management.
All are housed in a modest twelve-story stone building—the
Maiatico Building—on Washington's Connecticut Avenue.
The organization operates under the wing of the State De-
partment.

As the whole world seems to know, the Peace Corps is
headed by Robert Sargent Shriver, a 47-year-old, good-
looking six-footer. A Yale graduate, he helped to manage
Chicago's Merchandise Mart for Joseph Kennedy. He is
married to Kennedy's daughter Eunice; they have four
children.

He was extremely active in Chicago civic affairs, particularly in education, before taking on his Peace Corps assignment. For his present mission, he is said to be possessed
with an almost evangelical zeal, in fact, he has been described as a combination Billy Graham and the late Tom
Dooley, with a dash of advertising salesman added in.

Director Shriver has logged more than 500,000 miles in traveling to 40 of the 46 countries where volunteers are serving. He likes to find out for himself what the Peace Corps is doing. On these trips, he talks at length to volunteers, to citizens in remote areas, to newspapermen, to heads of state. He likes to be able to spot Peace Corps mistakes before outsiders do.

Early in 1964, speculation that Mr. Shriver might be chosen to run as Vice-Presidential candidate was heightened when Mr. Johnson appointed the Peace Corps Director to direct the administration's anti-poverty program, while retaining his Peace Corps responsibilities. In his new capacity, Sargent Shriver has the title of Special Assistant to the President in charge of the program's organization and administration. Since assuming office, President Johnson has found several occasions upon which to comment concerning Sargent Shriver's "outstanding qualities of leadership."

Astutely assisting Director Shriver is Deputy Director Bill Moyers, a bright, young (he's not yet 30), and brainy Texas-educated Oklahoman. Moyers came to Washington in 1954 as a special assistant to Senate Majority Leader Lyndon Johnson. His post was slated to be a temporary summer assignment. But Johnson, finding Moyers a brilliant idea man, asked him to stay on. He did; he found Washington and Washington politics to be "irresistible." The bespectacled Moyers came to be Johnson's executive assistant during the Senator's 1960 campaign for the vice-presidency and now he ranks as an important and extremely high-regarded presidential aide.

If Sargent Shriver has one special talent, it is his ability to get along with Congress. Early in 1961, he was granted a $30 million budget for the Peace Corps' first fiscal year of operation—$9.8 million for administrative costs, and $20.2 million for volunteer projects. This was at a time when no one was quite sure what the Peace Corps was, or what it intended to accomplish. For this beneficent Congressional treatment, President Kennedy praised him as "the most effective lobbyist in Washington."

For the fiscal year 1963, the Peace Corps requested $63.7 million and was granted $59 million, of which $43.5 million was earmarked for volunteer project costs, and $15.5 million for administrative charges. (According to Mr. Shriver, it costs about $9,000 to support one volunteer worker for one year.)

In his budget message to Congress covering fiscal year 1964, President Kennedy requested $108 million for Peace Corps activity. Eighty-one per cent of this money was tagged for volunteer and project costs; the balance for administrative expenses. Appearing before Congress in October, 1963, Sargent Shriver requested that his budget be revised downward to $102 million, in line with the decreased number of volunteers to be accepted for service. This move, remarkably unique among government agencies, served to enhance the already splendid image the Peace Corps holds among members of Congress.

Sargent Shriver claims a "special kind of person" is attracted to the Peace Corps organization. They came at the beginning, he says, and they still come. In his operational rounds, Director Shriver comes in contact with, not only Ph.D's and M.D.'s, but an occasional mountain climber or an ex-boxer and, once, a former smuggler. At staff meetings in Washington sit former members of state legislatures, union leaders, newspaper editors, farmers, college presidents, lawyers, psychiatrists, psychologists, and doctors.

Dr. Hobbs has published some of the most lucid and thoughtful comments on the type of person interested in (and accepted for) Peace Corps service. In one paper, he calls the volunteers "learners." Says Dr. Hobbs, "They have been reaching-out-type people and the Peace Corps experience is but a natural extension of the already developed pattern of intellectual adventuresomeness. They are terribly inquisitive about the world, in general, and, they are also well-adjusted people," Dr. Hobbs says. "They are enthusiastic."

This "adventuresomeness," coupled with a desire to secure the maturing and broadening experience that comes with two years service in an obscure foreign country, is probably the basic reason that young people clamor to join the Peace Corps. Though it seems secondary, another reason is idealism. Applicants for service appreciate the opportunity to "do something." Yet, as Dr. Hobbs points out, "Nothing annoys a volunteer more than to be told how great he is. Heroics are for an earlier generation."

Dr. Leonard J. Duhl, from the beginning a consulting psychiatrist to the Peace Corps from the National Institute of Mental Health, has found that the most successful volunteers are "motivated by a blending of altruistic idealism and the appropriate sense of self-seekingness." Dr. Duhl makes another important point: volunteers have decided, he says, "to work within the 'establishment'; they are not peace marchers or Freedom Riders." They want to be active, but within the framework of accepted social standards. The successes that can be generated by people of this nature, both in their two years service in foreign countries and in this country following their return from overseas, is now the subject of a minute study on the part of Peace Corps psychiatrists.

The type of person attracted to Peace Corps service, as described by the organization's psychiatrists, would seem to be ideally suited to the objectives of the Peace Corps program as a whole. For it is essentially a people-to-people service, not one that focuses upon a supply of technical or material resources. The volunteer is the central focus of this service, and as such, it is well he is a "learner," a "reaching-out" type person, whose motives for service express a well-adjusted admixture of ideal and reality.

CHAPTER 3

Selection
and
Training

As the Peace Corps idea began to take form and shape in the early months of 1961, Sargent Shriver and his gathering coterie of talent were faced with a personnel selection problem of dire proportions. From the tens of thousands of prospective volunteers who had written letters of query and who sought to make formal application, could the proper candidates be culled? No problem loomed as large as this one, for the Peace Corps' heartiest supporters and its most virulent critics both agreed that the organization could only be as good as its volunteers.

Criticism of the Peace Corps idea reached its greatest heights during the first months of 1961, and in their criticism, newspapers and magazines focused on the selection problem. *Time* magazine reported, "Skeptics at once envisioned pony-tailed coeds and crew-cut Jack Armstrongs playing Albert Schweitzer—an appalling army of innocents abroad." In the same publication, a picture of a training scene was captioned—with a lack of enthusiasm typical of early 1961—"They May Do More Good Than Harm."

The Wall Street Journal offered, editorially, the question, "What person . . . can really believe that Africa aflame with violence will have its fires quenched because some Harvard boy or Vassar girl lives in a mud hut and speaks Swahili?"

In March, 1961 Sargent Shriver appointed Dr. Nicholas Hobbs, Chairman of the Division of Human Development of the George Peabody College for Teachers in Nashville as the Director of Selection for the Peace Corps. Dr. Hobbs had been Chairman of the Division of Clinical Psychology of the American Psychological Association and during World War II, he helped to develop the U.S. Air Force's selection processes. Before he joined the Peace Corps, Dr. Hobbs served on the faculties of Columbia, Harvard, and the University of Pennsylvania, and he was, at one time, chairman of the Psychology Department at Louisiana State University. At that time, and today, he could be ranked as a formidable figure in his field.

Working with leading psychologists, educators, and personnel specialists and drawing upon the services offered by the Educational Testing Service of Princeton, New Jersey, Dr. Hobbs set the basic and general policy that recruitment was to be self-administered. As much as possible, volunteers were to be selected by means of comprehensive questionnaires and placement examinations. The policy exists today, in pretty much the same terms.

The Volunteer Questionnaire—to use its official title—is an extremely thorough, 12-page, brain-jogging request for information prepared in conjunction with the American Institute of Research. Completing the questionnaire is the sole method of making official application for Peace Corps service. At this stage, there are no personal interviews.

A letter to Peace Corps offices in Washington brings the applicant a questionnaire form within two weeks. (The inquiring applicant is also given a gratuitous subscription to *The Volunteer,* a slick-looking, slickly-produced monthly magazine containing Peace Corps project histories, volunteer interviews, post-service job and educational opportunities, and assistance and information requests from volunteers to other volunteers in search of know-how on everything from increasing the firing temperature of pottery to the construction of leg-pedaled boats.) At the present time applicants are advised not to submit questionnaires until one year before they wish to enter and are eligible for service. *The Volunteer Questionnaire* is also available at most Post Offices, at college Peace Corps liaison offices, or from United States Senators or Congressional representatives.

In addition to asking the expected questions as to address, birthdate, marital status ("if engaged," the questionnaire says "give name of fiance"), citizenship status, and the like, the applicant must detail his professional and educational background in great depth, and evaluate all of his technical experience, ranging from his ability to pilot an airplane to his talent at repairing communications equipment. In all, the prospective volunteer must grade himself in 204 skill areas.

The document begins with a personal message from Director Shriver and ends with a request for references. Peace Corps selection officials hold references in high regard. In depth information requests are sent to as many as 12 of the candidates former educational, business, professional, or military contacts. The request for personal and professional information about the candidate is accompanied by a personal letter from Director Shriver pointing up the patriotic responsibility on the part of the reference in providing complete and completely honest information as to the skills, character, and personality of the candidate. Selection officials say that this reminder of a person's moral obligation as a citizen has been an extremely effective means of obtaining fair, but very frank, words concerning a candidate's worth.

As soon as the questionnaires arrive in the Peace Corps' Washington selection offices, preliminary evaluation begins. A small percentage of applicants are rejected immediately; they are underage or otherwise not legally fit for service. Within a week, those who remain qualified are notified that the selection process is beginning and their references are being checked. In the first months of Peace Corps operation, for reasons of expediency, background investigations were handled by agents of the F.B.I., but today the U.S. Civil Service Commission oversees the job.

Candidates also must be medically and psychologically qualified. They are given thorough physical examinations at Federal medical facilities near their homes. (If they live more than 100 miles from a federal medical installation, their family physician is allowed to perform the medical check.) Like all the background information, the medical evaluations are sent to Washington Peace Corps headquarters to be analyzed. Six per cent of the candidates are rejected for medical reasons.

Some time during this initial evaluation stage, the candidate is asked to take a Placement Test, although for the first two years of Peace Corps operation the test was not mandatory. It is now, however. The Placement Examinations are given 12 times a year under the aegis of the U.S. Civil Service Commission and are designed to assist the selection division in the placement of individual applicants.

The test is divided into two parts, general aptitude and language aptitude, with testing pretty much limited to verbal and arithmetic ability, and to reasoning power. According to some of those who have taken the test, the best way to prepare for it is to brush up on grammar school arithmetic. In one section, applicants are given two minutes to memorize 24 "words" from the Kurdish language along with the English translations of these words. Then, the words must be used in answering specific questions.

By this time, the Peace Corps has a sizeable dossier on the prospective volunteer. It includes the results of the Placement Test, the information derived from *The Volunteer Questionnaire,* information from the candidate's references, and preliminary medical reports. Under a system organized by Dr. Lowell Kelly, a former President of the American Psychological Association, and currently Chairman of the Department of Psychology at the University of Michigan, the information is fed into computers where it is evaluated and assessed in the light of current and specific Peace Corps project needs. Selection officials stress that the computer does not make the final selection: the computer "nominates" trainees for particular programs, they say. Final decisions are made by selection officials.

If a candidate is found to meet the standards, a letter assigns him to a specific training group at a particular university. Only about one applicant in six is found suitable for training. For any one of a variety of reasons—physical, emotional, educational—candidates are rejected. But as the

number of applicants increases, the percentage of acceptable recruits is decreasing.

The entire selection process—from the receipt of the applicant's questionnaire in Washington headquarters to the
letter of acceptance—can be a lengthy process. At one time,
it could take a year or more, but now the Peace Corps is
more experienced in handling information and the process
generally takes two to three months. The goal is one month.
(One stunned applicant—in a much-needed job category—
was assigned to duty after a six-day wait.)

"Only about one-half of the applicants accept our invitation to train," says Frank Erwin, formerly Deputy Director
of Selection. "Partly, this is due to the time lag. The applicants we are after usually have career offers with business
and industry to consider or they are weighing educational
opportunities. Their status changes—some get married and
some look to continuing their education. By the time we
get around to assigning them, many of them have chosen
something else." Admittedly, this is one of the agency's
shortcomings; but, it is being licked.

In 1962, the Peace Corps launched a number of public
affairs and information programs to help stimulate applicant inquiries. Some of these programs achieved mild success; others, according to officials were "bombs." One, a
recruiting booth centered in the heart of Times Square,
was an exceptional failure.

Then, early in 1963, the Peace Corps initiated more
highly-organized, more pointed "information" programs.
Peace Corps officials claim to "inform" prospective volunteers; they shun the word "recruit." But no matter the
nomenclature, the programs are designed "to get the questionnaire." And remember they have met with splendid

success. The last few months of 1963 and the first few months of 1964 saw questionnaires coming into Peace Corps Washington headquarters at the rate of 150 a day— an all time high. During 1962, questionnaires were received at the rate of only 1,000 a month. In December, 1963, 4,807 questionnaires were received. An all time high was achieved in February, 1964: close to 6,000 questionnaires.

Peace Corps recruiting covers two prime areas. First, all colleges and universities—about 75 per cent of the effort, and second, all agricultural and technical professions. The Peace Corps maintains a harmonious working relationship with the nation's colleges and universities and boasts liaison officers—usually college administrative or placement officials—on 1,100 campuses. From these campus liaison officials, Peace Corps news items and general information are disseminated to the student body. Recruiting officials from Washington headquarters make periodic visits to most college campuses, and during the spring of the year, Sargent Shriver and other top-level Peace Corps officials are popular and willing commencement speakers.

Under a program developed at the University of Wisconsin in April, 1963, the Peace Corps now recruits from universities via the "Task Force" method. A particular city or a particular campus is selected for a major recruiting thrust. From Washington, Peace Corps officials are "dragged off their staff jobs" to join with a group of volunteer veterans, those who have completed two years of service, for a series of personal appearances that spearhead the campus campaign.

In New York City, a recruiting program in December, 1963, covered 94 colleges, technical and nursing schools, representing a total of 275,000 students. Information booths were established on all of the campuses, classroom talks were scheduled, all media—daily press, campus newspapers, radio, and TV—were covered by Peace Corps campaigners. Activity reached a peak with a three day set of appearances by Sargent Shriver. In all, more than 75 people took part in the campaign. It was a huge success.

"College students, though they're our prime targets, really aren't too well informed about the Peace Corps," says Robert L. Gale, Director of Recruiting. "I've seen students come up to a campus information booth and say, 'I'd like to join, but I'm getting a Liberal Arts degree.' They don't seem to realize that half the Peace Corps jobs overseas involve teaching tasks. Liberal Arts people are among the most-needed."

Mr. Gale's statement points up a pair of overriding problems that have dogged the Peace Corps recruiters from the early days of the organization. First, many people feel they are too poorly qualified to seek Peace Corps service; they feel their training and their skills are inadequate for Peace Corps tasks. Along with this theory, there exists in the minds of many the feeling that the Peace Corps is pretty exclusively reserved for the young, just-graduated-from-college set.

The second problem is at the other end of the scale. Many people feel that they are too highly trained or too highly skilled for Peace Corps work. For instance, people like the Director of Diagnostic Health Services for the City of Detroit or the Executive Director of New York State's Housing and Community Renewal Division feel their wide knowledge and background and experience just are not suited to the social-economic problems of the Nigerian jungle bush.

Volunteers who can teach, particularly in mathematics or science, are the most in demand. Most volunteer teachers have had no practical teaching experience. Though there are approximately 5,000 Peace Corps teachers presently involved in teaching duties, there are requests for 5,000 more from countries in Africa, Asia, and Latin America. Dean John Munro of Harvard says that "two years in the Peace Corps is more significant than a Rhodes scholarship."

One-fourth of the overseas volunteers are assigned to agricultural tasks, and they range in experience from youngsters who simply grew up on farms to soil experts with doctoral degrees. Selection officials prefer to have applicants with two years of college training for an overseas agricultural assignment. Activity in the Future Farmers of America, the Heifer Project, the National Grange, or a 4-H program is highly regarded.

Engineers are much in demand, too. They are desired for the construction of roads and bridges in Malaya, Peru, Brazil, and North Borneo. And they are needed for the construction of irrigation systems in Ecuador, public works in Tunisia, and for housing and school construction in Somalia, Gabon, Nepal, and east Pakistan. An engineering degree is required.

Nurses form a fourth category requested by host countries. Peace Corps Volunteer Registered Nurses work as staff nurses in mental or maternity or infectious disease hospitals, and sometimes in leprosaria. Their tasks are varied but preparation in mid-wifery is always expected. Doctors are much in demand, too. In Africa, says the Peace Corps, there is one physician for every 80,000 people.

The Peace Corps has had problems in attracting skilled surveyors, sanitarians, well-drillers, and heavy-duty diesel mechanics. Usually, however, willing applicants can be taught these tasks. More of a problem though is the recruitment of experienced engineers, geologists, and French and Spanish speaking mathematics and science teachers. These skills are difficult to teach and are constantly in demand.

"It may not be fully realized," says Ken Coffee, Peace Corps recruiting official, "but a great many Peace Corps jobs overseas serve to increase and broaden a person's career experience. We had an architect's project in Malaysia where Peace Corps volunteers had a hand in designing entire cities. In our African lawyers project, in Nigeria and Tanganyika, we had volunteers helping to establish complete judicial and administrative systems."

No matter what the precise nature of the volunteer's assignment—whether he be utilized as an educator or a farmer, as a health expert or an engineer—all prospective volunteers take part in an intensive ten to twelve weeks of schooling in the United States before going overseas. Though there is a lot to accomplish during this training period, the course of study is kept short. Volunteers are anxious to get overseas. They are imbued, according to Robert Hellawell, Deputy Associate Director for Peace Corps Volunteers, with a desire to accomplish a lot, and Peace Corps officials have found that long periods of training, especially if attempted in the host country, seriously impair volunteer morale.

The earliest plan for training Peace Corps Volunteers was quite broad, and many variations have been introduced since the late months of 1961. But, generally, the training seeks to give the volunteer a reservoir of applied skills, both for his specialized vocation in the field, and for the general problems of service that will confront him. Students are taught in groups according to the country to which they will be assigned.

Peace Corps training is a year round activity though most projects begin during the summer months—from mid-June through the end of August—coinciding with the availability of high school and college students through graduation. Also, college campus training facilities are more available to the Peace Corps during the summer months. Rutgers, the State College of New Jersey, located in New Brunswick, was the first university to house and train a Peace Corps volunteer contingent. In June, 1961, 62 volunteers—all of them men—were assembled at Rutgers to train for a Peace Corps project in Colombia. They studied Spanish, United States and Latin American culture, and they learned how to ride a horse.

In early 1964, the Peace Corps was maintaining contractual training arrangements with some 70 American colleges and universities. Peace Corps contracts are not considered money makers for schools, since the Corps pays —for ten weeks of housing and study—an average of $200 for each student per week. But training contracts lend prestige and, since they are scheduled most often during the summer months, give use to otherwise idle classrooms and dormitories. The Peace Corps college and university training sites represent a pretty fair cross section of American institutions of higher learning, though Peace Corps officials have admittedly shied away from universities in the South because of segregation policies. The University of Texas lost a Brazil-bound Peace Corps group to the University of Oklahoma for reasons of segregation.

Whenever possible, colleges seek to match the environment of the country for which the students are being trained. During 1962, 70 volunteers, in training at Columbia University's New York School of Social Work, used the slums of Harlem as a training ground for an assignment in urban Colombia. Members of an agricultural project, bound for French-speaking Guinea, in training at Dartmouth College received instruction in both language and farm techniques from French farmers north of the Canadian border in Montreal. Another training group, preparing for the rugged life in the rarefied air of the Himalayas of Nepal, camped high up in the Rocky Mountains.

The Peace Corps is having excellent training results with its Far East volunteers in courses of study at the University of Hawaii's Hilo campus on the Island of Hawaii. Here is the closest duplication of Asian culture within the United States, and future plans call for almost all trainees bound for Far East assignment to be schooled at the Hilo center.

It consists of two distinctly different training sites. The first is a pair of converted barracks-type hospital buildings located on the outskirts of Hilo. They are used for classroom study. The second site is more exotic. Located about 50 miles north of Hilo, along the coast, it is no more than a remote tropical valley—the Waipio Valley—framed by the sea on one side, and the often snow-capped Kohala Mountains on the other. Here, students bound for Indonesia and the Philippines and other Far East areas learn to grow rice and taro and to work with the Asian beast of burden, the Carabao. Here, too, the student is schooled in what is probably one of the most unique courses of study in all of American education: the construction of Nipa (palm or thatch) huts. In this setting, the trainee undergoes a transitional

diet change, from stateside meat and potatoes to the fish
and rice of the Far East.

After three weeks of training in the Waipio Valley, the
fledgling volunteer is skilled at manufacturing a dutch-
oven for baking a cake, making guava jelly, preparing rice
paddy beds, and killing and preparing a pig in the accepted manner of the Philippines. It is, as Sargent Shriver
dubbed it, "realistic."

No matter what college or university to which he is assigned, the volunteer's course of study is an intense and
vigorous one. It averages 10-hours a day, six days a week. In
addition, during the student's free time, the sponsoring
university tries to expose him to as many of the social and
cultural mores of the host country as possible. For instance,
Peace Corps groups bound for Nigeria and training at
Columbia University's New York School of Social Work
are supplied with opportunities to mix with students of the
university who are citizens of Nigeria.

Courses of study vary widely. "They are more different
than alike," says Dr. William Craig, Peace Corps Director
of Training. Their make-up depends on the country and
the type of project for which candidates are training. But,
basically, they include a course in Technical Studies, that
is, instruction in the skills of the job for which the candidate is to be assigned. For instance, a trainee assigned to an
Agricultural Reform program in Panama will be taught
the hows and whys of crop rotation and pig-penning. Technical Studies generally make up 15 to 20 per cent of the
curriculum.

In addition, the trainee is instructed in the historical,
political, economic, and cultural aspects of both the United
States and the host country to which he is being assigned.

There is a special course in World Affairs that includes a look at Communist strategy and tactics. Health and medical training are other courses of study.

Language training is all-important and in most courses, it is given the bulk of attention. At first it was thought that the exotic languages—Thai, Urdu, Bengali, Twi, and the like—would offer the greatest training problems. This theory hasn't held true, for volunteers who show only the slightest fluency in languages such as Thai are tremendously appreciated by the citizenry for their modest achievement. On the other hand, volunteers in Spanish-speaking Latin America and in French colonies in Africa are criticized because they often possess only a mediocre knowledge of Spanish or French. In these languages, the Peace Corps has found, citizen-like fluency is expected.

When a student is confronted with an obscure dialect, the training problem can be immense. This can best be illustrated with this excerpt from the syllabus on "Teaching in Secondary Schools in Nigeria," as developed by the Teachers College at Columbia University:

"Hausa is part of the Chadic subbranch of the Afro-Asiatic language family (formerly called Hamito-Semitic). Despite the fact that it is non-Indo-European, its ultimate affiliation with Hebrew and Arabic (from which it borrowed many words) will probably make it easier for you than anticipated. Apart from the acquisition of vocabulary, the peculiar difficulties that Hausa presents are the pronunciation and the tense-aspect system of verbs (which is formed essentially by change of tones)."

The Peace Corps is proud of the fact that its university training centers offer some of the only courses of instruction in the United States in such obscure languages and dialects as Amharic, Bengali, Ewe, Twi, Tagalog, Urdu, and Yoruba. And the organization takes further pride in the knowledge that basic teaching methods and basic texts in some of these tongues, some of them with absolutely no previous written tradition at all have been developed by Peace Corps sponsored instructors.

During 1963, many of the university courses of study became extremely elaborate and sophisticated. The aforementioned Columbia University Training Program for teaching in secondary schools in Nigeria is one example. Stretching to 12 weeks, it ranks as one of the Peace Corps' very best.

Sixty hours of the first four weeks are given over to African Studies and Language Studies, including a look at the rise and development of African nationalism, the traditional background of present day Africa and the early European contacts of the continent. Instructors in this area, as in all other portions of the program, are of the highest caliber. L. Gray Cowan heads the African Studies course of study. He holds an A.B. from Toronto and an A.M. and Ph.D. from Columbia University. A student of African politics since 1950, he has traveled extensively through the continent. He is a ranking member of various African study groups and the author of *West African Local Government* as well as a host of articles on the politics of Africa.

Karl W. Bigelow, Executive Officer of the Institute for Education in Africa, holds an A.B. and L.H.D. from Clark University, a Ph.D. from Harvard University, and an LL.D. from Parsons University. A student of African education since 1949, he has visited British-related West, Central, and East Africa, the Republic of South Africa and the Sudan, and he is the author of books and articles relating to general education, teacher education, and African education. Bright and articulate, he boasts a very great knowledge of African educational affairs.

In all, 40 scholars and teachers, all of them remarkably well-qualified, have been brought together to prepare the trainees for Peace Corps work in Nigeria. R. Freeman Butts, Director of International Studies at Columbia Teachers College, has said that it is likely "that no comparable array of talent has been marshalled outside of Nigeria with as much recent and first-hand knowledge of Nigeria and its schools." There seems no reason to dispute Mr. Butts.

Other colleges and universities offer training programs of equal merit, both academically and in the presentation of the environment the volunteer will be facing. The University of New Mexico is highly regarded in the training and education it has performed for volunteers bound for Community Development work in Colombia. Heavy on field work, the program schools trainees in rural Spanish areas of New Mexico where urban redevelopment and social welfare problems can be learned firsthand.

At one time, the University of Massachusetts, at Amherst, presented a training program unique for its diversity. It, first, provided coaches of boxing, basketball, swimming, track and field, and tennis; coaches who, in turn, trained regional and national teams in Senegal and the Ivory Coast. Second, the program furnished building construction foremen, farm machinery mechanics, and foremen for irrigation and well-digging projects; these supervisors assisted in the rural training schools of Senegal. Third, the program trained volunteer agriculture extension workers for service in Niger.

The University of Wisconsin trained volunteers for India in 12-week, 60-hour-a-week schedules, of which 50 per cent of the time was given over to language training in Hindi-Urdu with students becoming proficient enough to read and converse in the tongue.

Small colleges as well as large have served as training sites. Volunteers bound for Ghana, India, Panama, Bolivia, and Ethiopia have received schooling at the University of California, the country's largest. The highly regarded and prestigious University of Michigan's center for Far East Studies trained volunteers for Thailand. Colleges less grandiose that are utilized have included Berea, where volunteers for Senegal are trained; Montana State College, where Ecuador bound volunteers have received instruction; and Springfield College, in Springfield, Massachusetts, which has been used for projects in Ecuador and Venezuela.

In the mountains south of Arecibo in Puerto Rico, the Peace Corps maintains and operates the only training installation it can call its own. It consists of two "outward bound" camps, Camp Crozier and Camp Radley. Carved out of rugged mountain jungle area, each of these camps offers a four-week course, almost purely physical in makeup, and comparable in many ways to a World War II Army basic training center or Navy boot camp.

The curriculum in Puerto Rico consists of three main courses: Trekking, Rock Climbing, and Swimming and Lifesaving. Trainees—both men and women—must be able to sustain themselves in a deep water swim pool for 45 minutes under a system of "drown-proofing," developed by onetime Peace Corps swim coach, Fred Lanoue. Volunteers must be able to trek through jungle wilderness three to four days, subsisting largely on bananas, but also on handouts from native villagers. They must try to scale a hundred-foot sheer rock cliff.

A University of Florida psychologist, Dr. Sidney M. Jourard, has written extensively about the camp and the effects it imposes on the trainees. Here is an excerpt from one of his reports, describing a routine day at Camp Crozier:

"Awakened at 6:00 A.M., by Jim Lowry, the PE instructor and by 6:15, the whole camp was out for physical jerks. Very vigorous. Instructors set a good example, getting on to the muddy ground with everyone. Culminates in (for me) an exhausting run of about a half mile, ending at mess hall. I was trembling so from the run that I could barely eat the huge breakfast that was available. The same was true of many of the trainees. All the trainees now in camp garb—dungarees, work-shirts, Spanish boots. After breakfast, our group had drown-proofing in the pool. One of the trainees, an older fellow in his forties, expressed the hope that the athletics wouldn't overtax an old 're-tread' like himself. Drown-proofing consists of relaxing in the water, keeping face submerged, and with minimum effort, raising face for breath, rhythmically, as needed. Permits one to stay in water indefinitely. After about an hour at it, I found myself thinking what a marvelous tranquilizer the experience was. The deeper exhalation and inhalation makes one have the experience of being 'fully present,' with empty mind—like Yogi breathing exercises. Majority of the trainees in our group mastered the technique quickly.

"Spanish class followed drown-proofing. Our instructor

was very patient, a Cuban fellow Felix Lopez, with much experience at teaching conversational Spanish. I find myself learning rudimentary Spanish quickly.

"After lunch, we went for 'Rocks.' The instructor, a stocky, husky fellow, Ben Elkus, gave a good lecture about the philosophy of 'outward-bound,' of the role of rock-climbing; elicited fears from the group about heights, ropes breaking, lack of trust in the fellow holding the rope. Then we broke up in smaller groups to learn a couple of knots used in climbing, the bowline, and the fisherman's knot for binding two ropes together.

"After 'Rocks,' we went on five-mile trek led by Anita, the wife of the swim-instructor, a lovely, slim, blonde girl. She pointed out various edible and harmful roots, plants, fruits, viz: breadfruit, malanga, guava, yautea, inge, casi and robino. The scenery on this trek was breathtaking. Noted the Puerto Rican farm homes, shabby from outside, impeccable inside, 21-inch TV in most, over-run with children, the younger males usually naked, or with shirts, but no pants.

"Evening program time, after supper, devoted to a planning for subsequent evening programs. Later, group went to Tomasito's. I brought my guitar, and we sang."

Trainees, throughout the entire program are encouraged, but not forced, to extend themselves to their utmost—and then a little bit more. Though the program may be rugged, it provides an especially gratifying experience by strengthening the trainees' emotional resources through the exploitation of physical stress situations. Trainees are high in their praise of the program.

Only about 30 per cent of all trainees are assigned to the

Puerto Rico regimen. Each camp can handle 100 volunteers at a time, and therefore it is not possible to schedule every prospective volunteer through this training phase.

Dr. Craig stresses that the Puerto Rico training procedure, though largely physical, is also practical, for as a second phase of the training program, volunteers are assigned to live with poor rural Puerto Rican families. (One volunteer described them as "super-poor.") In this way, trainees receive both language and community development experience.

About midway through the training program, a field selection board is convened to evaluate each candidate individually. The board is made up of a doctor, a psychologist, the trainee's teachers, the group's training officer, and a representative of the host country. Then, at the end of the training program, a final advisory selection meeting is held. One of three recommendations is made concerning each candidate: First, the trainee is assigned overseas with the group; or, second, the trainee is separated from the group and perhaps recommended for another project. Or, third, the trainee may be separated from the Peace Corps.

Two of ten candidates, to use Sargent Shriver's phrase, are "selected out." The reasons for recommended separation are diverse. Scholastically or physically the candidate may not measure up. More often, he is found to be weak in stress situations of the type he will face overseas. The change in "life style," with the concomitant periods of homesickness and frustration may be judged to be too severe for him. The recommendations are made by the board to its chairman and to the field selection officer; he determines final action.

As the Peace Corps has become more experienced in

selection and training, the psychologist has come to have a more responsible part of the program. There is now one psychiatrist available for each group of 50 trainees. Appointed by and employed by the university, he instructs the trainees in mental health; he observes the trainee in formal and in informal situations.

There have been charges that the Peace Corps "wastes manpower" in some of its overseas assignments, though the charge is much less likely to hold true today than in late 1961 and early 1962. Selection and training methods have been substantially improved since the first training group arrived on the Rutgers campus in June, 1961. *The Volunteer Questionnaire* has been expanded. The Placement Test has been rendered more definitive (though it has been shortened) and taking the placement exam is now mandatory. Training sites—colleges and universities—present programs of greater depth than once was the case. The final decision on a candidate's worth is more elaborate, more precise. And the entire process has been hastened by the use of automated selection methods.

CHAPTER 4

The
Volunteer
Overseas

SARGENT SHRIVER's precepts for working effectively overseas are few and simple. "First," he says, "learn the language of the people. Second, make up your mind that the work of developing nations is worth the price of personal sacrifice. Third, anchor yourself in the customs and traditions of the country where you are serving, get down to 'eye level' with the people. Fourth, believe in the power of personal integrity, humility, and determination."

Early in 1964, more than 8,000 Peace Corps volunteers, serving in 47 countries of every developing continent, were seeking to carry out Director Shriver's words.

Geographically, the Peace Corps overseas operation is divided into four major areas. The largest is the Latin American program; next, is Africa (south of the Sahara); third, the Far East, and fourth, a single program embracing the Near East, South Asia, and North Africa.

The type of program assigned to a particular country is a good reflection of the socio-economic structure of the area.

(Countries make specific requests as to the type of volunteer and type of program they require.) In Latin America, where abject poverty and disease are so common as to be regarded with indifference, program emphasis is on rural community action. In Africa, where a dozen new nations seek the intellectual stimulus so necessary to the responsibilities of self-government, the emphasis is on education—education on all levels.

The same theory applies to individual countries: mountainous, unmapped Tanganyika needs surveyors; undeveloped Ghana requests geological engineers; dry and barren Morocco wants irrigation experts; Thailand, studded with jungle rain forests, seeks experts in malaria control; crop-poor St. Lucia wants agricultural experts.

The Latin American program, with approximately 3,000 volunteers in 18 countries, is largely involved in community development work in rural areas. Volunteers are helping to build schools, roads, and health clinics and attempting to encourage villagers and slum dwellers to organize themselves and their resources for their own betterment. Most attention in Latin American countries has been given to Colombia. It was the first Latin American country to receive volunteers, and though early attempts at development work in that country were sometimes greeted by apathy and even bitterness, results in recent months have been a great deal more favorable. Late in 1963, there were more than 400 volunteers in service in or in training for Colombia.

Peru has received much attention, too. More than 400 volunteers are involved in Peruvian projects, serving as construction tradesmen, social workers, and sanitarians in helping the people of the "barriadas" to build decent housing and improve living conditions. In addition, volunteers in Peru teach carpentry, masonry, and electrical skills. In Bolivia, the Peace Corps has provided civil engineers and construction workers as well as volunteers with agricultural skills.

Programs in rural western Venezuela are concerned with agricultural assistance and home economics instruction. There is a Venezuelan educational program, with volunteers engaged in the instruction of English in such places as Caripito, Cumana, and Carupano—not exactly bulging urban areas. But volunteers also teach, mainly English and Science, at colleges in metropolitan Caracas.

Rural education, urban renewal, and urban development are the principal projects in Chile and the Dominican Republic. Along Brazil's long Sao Francisco Valley, volunteers are assisting in a TVA-type project that will help to better living conditions for more than five million people. Sanitation and Public Health workers are busy in Panama, Honduras, and St. Lucia. In Jamaica, in a program that had some sharp but brief growing pains, volunteers are helping to train that 20 per cent of the island's work force that is chronically unemployed. Volunteers are introducing new agricultural techniques to the farmers of Panama, Guatemala, Uraguay, and El Salvador.

In the first months of Peace Corps activity, the greatest number of volunteers were sent to assignments in developing nations of Africa in an effort to help supply the tremendous need for school teachers and school builders in these newly independent nations. Approximately 2,500 volunteers now serve in 17 African countries, and Peace Corps headquarters in Washington has received requests for at least twice that many.

The largest volunteer program in Africa is centered in Nigeria, and Peace Corps teachers are now represented in more than 15 per cent of Nigeria's schools. The instruction is generally on the secondary school level. Volunteers for Nigeria are exceptionally well trained; their responsibilities in the educational development of the country are heavy. In fact, officials of the government of the country have described their work as "indispensable."

Twelve of the 17 programs in Africa are basically teaching programs. In Ghana, Peace Corps volunteers constitute more than a third of the degree-holding instructors in the country's secondary schools. In Ethiopia and Nyasaland, more than a third of all teachers are volunteers. Peace Corps educational assistance is not always of purely an instructional nature; in Gabon, working in concert with the Agency for International Development, Peace Corps volunteers have constructed five entire schools.

Volunteers in educational projects in Africa have helped to establish the first secondary school system in West Cameroon; have assisted in the introduction of English language instruction course in the schools of the Ivory Coast; have influenced the Liberian government toward increasing education expenditures by 25 per cent; have taught the English language in French to 30 per cent of Niger's secondary school students.

In addition to lending educational assistance in Tanganyika, a volunteer project of surveyors, engineers, and geologists have helped to build a network of farm-to-market roads, mapped out almost 7,000 square miles of land for mineral surveys, and worked on harbors, bridges, and drainage systems. On other projects in Africa, architects and nurses and mechanics serve in Tunisia; doctors and fishermen in Togo, and agricultural specialists in Senegal. In the Far East, where about 1,500 volunteers serve, teaching programs also predominate. The biggest single project in the Far East, in fact, the biggest in the entire Peace Corps operation, is at work in the Philippines. Here, more than 600 volunteers teach in 350 rural elementary schools. But teaching is only a part of their responsibility; they have an active role in "barrio" life. Volunteers have proved effective in community development work, in developing recreational programs, in garden planning and cultivation, and in the construction of sanitary facilities.

In Thailand, volunteers serve in a wide range of areas. Laboratory technicians work on medical diagnoses problems in provincial hospitals and in malaria eradication programs. Similar medical programs are under way in North Borneo and Sarawak where the variety of assignment extends to livestock raising and general veterinary care.

In Malaya, more than half of the volunteers are teachers. In Indonesia, volunteers serve as physical education instructors.

In the Near East and South Asia program, about 900 volunteers serve in eight countries. In Pakistan, where requests for volunteers has passed the 1,000 mark, the Peace Corps has been in operation since November, 1961. Volunteers are on duty as teachers and nurses, and in programs concerned with agriculture, public health, and rural public works. Peace Corps volunteers are held in high esteem in Pakistan and are often consulted on matters involving national development policies.

India, with its staggering social and economic needs, presents the Peace Corps with an enormous challenge toward making really significant contributions. There are about 150 volunteers in service in India. They work on agricultural extension and rural housing projects; they work on town planning and small business improvement. They are involved in youth work. They teach.

There are volunteer printers and mechanics in Afghanistan. In Nepal, volunteers brought farm animals 300 miles from Kathmandu to a small mountain village to start a livestock project. In Cyprus, five Peace Corps geologists prepared a detailed map that will help the government in its planning for more effective use of water and mineral resources. Also in Cyprus, Ceylon, Afghanistan, Iran, Nepal, and Turkey, Peace Corps volunteers teach—mostly on a secondary school level.

In nature and in location, the assignments cover a wide range. Basil Stergios, of Harvard, Massachusetts, serves in Cayambe, Ecuador, only three miles from the Equator. Kathy Abitz, of Schofield, Wisconsin, and Nancy Crawford of East Providence, Rhode Island, have received the highest assignment; they operate a health clinic in the Andean village of El Alto, 13,414 feet above sea level. Robert Unger serves in Restauracion in the Dominican Republic, less than 700 miles from his home in Miami. But Mr. and Mrs. Marvin Adams, of Huntington, Indiana, are working for the Peace Corps in an especially remote village, 250 miles up the Kinabatangan River in North Borneo. They are five days from civilization by outboard motor boat; by radio, they are in contact with the outside world only twice a week.

Each country's Peace Corps program is supervised and directed by a field leader in the country who is directly responsible to the American ambassador. Generally, these are men in their late thirties or early forties, who have attained a good amount of stature in educational fields, or in social science work, or in government or privately-sponsored assistance programs.

William G. Saltonstall, for 17 years principal of the prestigious Phillips Exeter Academy, Exeter, New Hampshire, and one of the most respected educators in America, is Peace Corps administrator for Nigeria. In Ethiopia, Peace Corps programs were supervised by Harris Wofford, a onetime special assistant to President Kennedy, and author of the book, *India Afire*. Early in 1964, he was named Associate Director for Planning and Evaluation. Directing the Peace Corps program in Iran is Dr. William J. Cousins, former Chief of the Training and Resources Branch of the Agency for International Development. Heading Peace Corps activity in Bolivia is Derek Singer, who has worked with both CARE and AID, and served as one of the members of Sargent Shriver's organizational "Task Force" in the early days of 1961. In the Philippines, Peace Corps Representative was Dr. Lawrence Fuchs, Dean of Faculty at Brandeis University, and a noted author and lecturer on foreign affairs. Other countries and other projects are staffed with Peace Corps Representatives of almost equal merit.

In addition to supervisors who reflect a general excellence, volunteers are provided skilled medical support in their overseas assignments. There are currently more than 50 doctors from the U.S. Public Health Service on assignment in project countries to oversee the volunteer's medical needs. In addition, the Peace Corps approves certain host country physicians and hospitals where volunteer medical care can be sought.

The volunteer program of medical care emphasizes preventive measures, seeking to allay the onset of the most
common volunteer ailments. These include upper respira-
tory infections, brought on by changes in climate and the
sometimes severe stepdown in the quality of the volunteer's housing and shelter. Skin complaints and dysentery
are frequent, resulting from a general lack of sanitation.
Infectious hepatitis and amoebiasis are other volunteer
health hazards.

East Pakistan has a prevalence of bovine tuberculosis.
Malaria is Ghana's biggest killer; volunteers sleep under
tightly drawn nets and take anti-malaria pills. In India,
almost every volunteer has suffered dysentery. In Chile,
each member of an early Peace Corps project lost an average of fifteen pounds because of an inadequate diet.

Six volunteers have died in service; four in plane crashes,
one from a liver ailment, the sixth from a jeep accident.
(Medical officials report that jeep accidents on bad roads
are a greater hazard to volunteer's life and limb than disease.)

Homesickness and loneliness are two burning problems
that volunteers face. One female volunteer wrote from
Africa, ". . . every once in a while we pull out the encyclo-
pedia to look at pictures of snowy New England. We eat
tons of peanut butter because it is so super-markety-Ameri-
can to us."

In his on-site investigations, Sargent Shriver has found
that morale of the Peace Corps volunteer is best where
conditions are the hardest. "Where we have difficulty overseas is not in a small village on the side of a mountain in a
remote place in Colombia, but in Bogota: it's not in Udon
on the Laotian border in Thailand, but in Bangkok: it's

not in the Philippine village of Talibon, but in Manila. Wherever the living is easy or the working conditions seem rather pleasant, that's where the Peace Corps runs into trouble."

A volunteer who lives in a Nipa hut in the Borneo jungle, carries his water from a jungle stream, boils it to make it potable, eats little but fish and rice, and teaches the fundamentals of the English language to groups of ragged native children, often develops a deep-seated zeal toward his work assignment. This is how he imagined Peace Corps life would be. He feels his assignment has real purpose; he is making a contribution. The social and physical discomforts he experiences increase his drive, and his desire to succeed.

But consider the volunteer stationed in a three-room air-conditioned apartment in Sao Paulo, Brazil, a sophisticated South American metropolis with more than two million people; one who works a seven-and-one-half hour day teaching Brazilian electrical engineers. His greatest emotional outpouring may come from the fact that he judges he is terribly underpaid. He may even come to feel his Peace Corps activity is a waste.

Peace Corps volunteers in remote overseas assignments are also subject to a rather unique malady, now commonly known as "culture shock." Rather an updated version of homesickness, it occurs to volunteers who undergo a gradual and subtle diminishing of familiar symbols. It manifests itself by a state of unhappiness and frustration. "Culture shock, and problems of homesickness and loneliness, are usually most prevalent in the first or second month of a volunteer's tour-of-duty," says Dr. Joseph G. English, Chief Psychiatrist for the Peace Corps.

"Periods of depression usually begin to develop right at the outset," Dr. English says. "A volunteer is often terribly surprised by the greeting he receives from the community in which he is to serve. Sometimes, because of lack of communication within the country, the people don't know the volunteer is coming. This is a major disappointment to the volunteer. In addition, many of the villagers, once they learn the volunteer is from America, expect him to immediately produce great wealth and make them all citizens of affluence. When the volunteer does not do this," Dr. English explains, "they are often disappointed in him."

These examples, and others like them, bring on periods of anxiety and depression for the volunteers. They feel they have failed personally, Dr. English says. "It's during this period that volunteers lose their Messianic complex. They have to make a reevaluation of their status and set to work becoming a part of the community." When they do this, they become valued Peace Corps members.

The discomforts produced by and expressed in the term "culture shock" are varied. Volunteers, in their individual work assignments, often lead quite solitary lives. Isolation can become a problem. Paradoxically, another adverse reaction can be produced by the constant scrutiny under which some volunteers are placed. Whether at work or not, volunteers never cease representing the Peace Corps. Often, they must lead a fish bowl–type existence.

Customs of personal hygiene on the part of the native population, the lack of sanitary facilities, and an overall tolerance for noise and dirt can become a source of strain for the volunteer. So can local sexual customs and rules of modesty in clothing.

Communication can be a serious psychological problem.

Not only may there be a normal language barrier, but a volunteer, even after becoming somewhat adept in the native tongue, may find it difficult to be understood. Words like "democratic" or "clean" or "soon" may have different meanings than he imagines.

"A second psychiatric crisis besets the volunteer after the first year or so," Dr. English states. "This is a result of a maturation of ideals; the challenge is gone." The volunteer feels if he were to spend the rest of his lifetime in the village in which he is working, he would not be able to solve 1 per cent of its problems. "It's at this stage the volunteer writes angry letters to Mr. Shriver and to the President," Dr. English says.

Dr. English and his Peace Corps colleagues seek to "inoculate" the volunteers emotionally against culture shock and other neuro-psychiatric disorders that may befall them. The problems brought on by isolation, by constant scrutiny, by living in conditions of forced intimacy, by strange food and living patterns are discussed with the volunteer before he is assigned overseas. "Face up to these reactions and discuss them with your friends," advises Sargent Shriver in a message to the overseas-bound volunteer.

Of course, the Peace Corps has no easy set of rules to cope with loneliness, homesickness, and frustration. But the fact that the agency recognizes that the problems exist is a giant step forward toward solving them. No such cognizance has ever been afforded any other American overseas personnel.

At one time, psychiatric counsel was used only in the selection of volunteers to screen out those applicants who it was felt would be ineffective overseas or susceptible to mental breakdown. However, for the past year the most

advanced concepts of behavioral sciences have been used
in every area of volunteer service, in selection, in training,
and in the assessment of the volunteer's overseas achieve-
ments. Today, the psychiatrist is an integral part of the
Peace Corps team, not (to use a term of Dr. Gerald Caplan's) just a "screener out." (Dr. Caplan, with Dr. Duhl,
both of the National Institute of Mental Health, have been
in the forefront in developing Peace Corps medical and
psychiatric policies.)

In no other government agency, and in extremely few
areas of business and industry, does the psychiatrist play
such a dominant role as he does in the Peace Corps. The
credit for this goes to Sargent Shriver. On a 1963 inspection
tour of Peace Corps facilities in the Far East, Director
Shriver was accompanied by a Peace Corps psychiatrist. It
raised some eyebrows. Explained Dr. Joseph Colmen, Peace
Corps Research Director, "Sargent Shriver often takes a
psychologist or psychiatrist with him. It's simply recog-
nition that we think of a volunteer's health in mental as
well as physical terms."

Peace Corps psychiatrists are now involved in a comprehensive program of research to determine precisely how
and why volunteers have performed as they have. They
plan to report on changes in the volunteer's own personality as a result of his overseas assignment, and they
plan to explain the changes the volunteer has been able to
effect in the country in which he has served. And, also,
they are looking into the just-developing problem of "re-
verse culture shock"—what happens when a volunteer who
has spent two years in a remote overseas assignment returns
to the United States.

Despite the assorted medical and mental problems that

volunteers face, the attrition rate among the membership has been strikingly low. Overseas it has been less than 2 per cent—a figure that never fails to amaze people with long experience in Peace Corps–type activity. Some early planning documents stated an expectancy of from 15 to 50 per cent attrition overseas. The 2 per cent figure experienced by the Peace Corps is one of its most apparent marks of success.

Many credit this triumph to the tested and proven selection process. Others say it is a result of the rigid, carefully-controlled training program. Finally, credit is given to the fact that psychiatric evaluation permeates the entire selection-training process. Dr. Hobbs may have the answer. Volunteers, he says, "in times of just manageable strain have gained new strength from a resolve not to let the Peace Corps down."

Beginning in June, 1963, the first volunteers on overseas assignment completed their two years of service and returned to the United States and, by January of the following year, close to a thousand volunteers had returned from 12 countries in Africa, Asia, and Latin America. They found that career opportunities abounded for them in education, in industry, and in government service.

Approximately half of the volunteers returning choose to continue their education, and they have a bewildering number of educational fellowships to choose from. Here are some examples.

—Stanford University's center for Comparative Education has established two assistantships for graduate study in Developmental Education.

—Yale University has announced that it is interested in having volunteers "apply for admission and financial aid."

Several fellowships have been set aside for returning volunteers by Yale.

—The University of Pittsburgh's Graduate School of Public and International Affairs is offering fellowships and special financial aid to volunteers.

—Harvard University's Graduate School of Education has set aside three tuition scholarships for volunteers.

—Arizona State University's Indian Education Center has set aside two graduate assistantships for volunteers.

This is only a small sampling. The list is long—and growing.

Almost every branch of government clamors for returning volunteers. President Kennedy expressed the hope that many former members of the Peace Corps would continue in government service—particularly in the U.S. Foreign Service. On orders from the late President, volunteers receive a preference rating on federal jobs.

The Department of State hopes that the Peace Corps will come to serve as kind of a recruiting service in staffing its overseas mission. Peace Corps volunteers, who do receive Foreign Service appointments, enter the agency at an advanced level.

Edward R. Murrow, former Director of the U.S. Information Agency, personally expressed a hope that volunteers would consider careers with his agency. The Surgeon General of the United States stated that he is "anxious" to recruit volunteers for service with the U.S. Public Health Service. The Department of Commerce, the Bureau of Indian Affairs, the Atomic Energy Commission, the Civil Service Commission, the U.S. Department of Agriculture —these, and other agencies of the government seek to recruit volunteers after separation.

From business and industry, the demand is almost as great. The country's biggest blue chip corporations have announced job opportunities for volunteers, principally in foreign markets. They feel that two years of overseas service is prime experience.

E. I. duPont has announced scores of openings in locations throughout the world for volunteers. International Minerals and Chemical Corporation wants volunteers for Africa and India; Ralston Purina Company wants them for the same countries. The First National City Bank has overseas banking posts for returnees. IBM, the Stauffer Chemical Corporation, and a host of other companies seek them.

Late in 1963, the Peace Corps, working with the American Council on Education, established the Peace Corps Volunteer Career Information Service. Headed by Robert Calvert, it assists volunteers with their post–Peace Corps planning. And the agency also serves as a clearing house for educational institutions and prospective employers who are seeking volunteer personnel.

CHAPTER 5

Projects
and
Programs

Introduction

The Peace Corps is now in full operation in 47 countries throughout the world. The nine programs evaluated in this chapter are those that, generally, have been in operation the longest period of time—since the final months of 1961 or the early months of 1962.

Some of the programs selected for study here were chosen because they are fairly typical ones. For instance, the Nigerian and Ethiopian teaching programs are similar in scope and size to the teaching programs in some of the other African nations. The Community Development work in Colombia and Bolivia is greatly similar to that in other South American countries where the Peace Corps is on assignment.

Some programs were chosen, too, because of their size and significance—the program in the Philippines, for example.

The Peace Corps programs in St. Lucia, Pakistan, Turkey, and Tanganyika were selected for study because of unique aspects of Peace Corps activity they present.

Bolivia

"The philosophy behind America's Peace Corps program has puzzled some of the people of Bolivia," says Ben Brackin, 20, of Oskaloosa, Iowa. He reports that Bolivia is glad to have the Peace Corps workers and that the people are anxious to learn from them, but that many fail to understand that the Americans came to help rather than to make money. But to the 150 Peace Corps volunteers serving in long-neglected and restless Bolivia, repairing the image of the "Norte Americanos" happens to be incidental to the work they are doing.

The volunteers are helping to build roads through jungles, and to plant coffee, rubber, citrus fruits, bananas, and cocoa. They operate an experimental farm which is testing new crops in an effort to expand and diversify the country's tin-dominated economy. Volunteers teach preventive medicine. In schools, they teach reading and writing. (Bolivia is a country where more than 70 per cent of the people are illiterate.) Volunteer nurses are helping to establish rural health clinics and dispensaries in areas that have relied on "cuarinderos"—witch doctors—for generations.

Operations in Bolivia are directed by Derek Singer, 34, who has previously worked with both CARE and AID programs in Latin America. He calls the volunteers the most "gung-ho" group of workers he has ever seen. Mr. Singer was one of the original members of Sargent Shriver's

Peace Corps "Task Force," the organizational group that convened in February–March, 1961.

Bolivia, about the size of Texas and California combined, is a country of slightly more than three million people. Though geographically tropical, the heart of the country is a vast, windy, treeless plateau called "El Altiplano," located two miles and more above sea level. Here are located most of the people and most of the cities. The altitude makes for assorted physical discomforts, among them shortness of breath. Volunteers, arriving from the United States at the La Paz airport, are met by medical assistants bearing oxygen tanks.

Beginning in 1538, and continuing for more than 400 years, a large share of Bolivia was owned and controlled by a Spanish-speaking minority. The present day social and economic ills of the country were spawned in those centuries, and though independence was achieved as early as 1825, the wealth of the country remained in the hands of a few families. Today poverty is widespread. The average annual per capita income is a meager $84.

In 1951, the government of Victor Paz Estenssaro was voted into power and proceeded to nationalize the tin mines and revamp the land tenure system. Since that time, except for a four year hiatus beginning in 1956, the Estenssaro government has been locked in a dire struggle to improve the country industrially and agriculturally.

The health of the country has deteriorated as the economy, and a great deal of Peace Corps assistance is directed toward improving health and sanitation practices of the country. Registered Peace Corps nurses administer inoculations and assist local doctors in surgery. They teach in nursing schools in La Paz, Sucre, and Tarija. Community development workers help prepare towns and villages for public health programs by teaching the basic rudiments of hygiene, sanitation, and nutrition. Licensed practical nurses help establish new health clinics and serve in those now existing.

Two volunteers serving as practical nurses are Nancy Ellen Crawford of East Providence, Rhode Island, and Kathy Abitz of Schofield, Wisconsin. Both are 21. They serve among the Aymara Indians, a race whose heritage goes back to the Inca empire, and are stationed high in the Andes mountain tableland, 13,500 feet above sea level, in the town of El Alto. The Aymaras, pushed up on this windswept wasteland by the Spanish conquerers, are today a sullen, withdrawn, and even hostile people.

"The Indians were very suspicious of us when we first arrived," Nancy recalls. "They have not trusted white people for centuries, but they became friendly as they saw we could make their sick babies smile and relieve their own suffering. They all accept us now," she says, "except the local witch doctor."

The two girls established a one-room health clinic at nearby Penas, a village of 4,000 people. It is furnished by a kerosene stove, one table, and several benches. Its construction was a marvel of international cooperation: the people of Penas volunteered to gather rocks for the foundation and make the adobe walls; the Peace Corps put on the roof and poured the cement floor; the Maryknoll Fathers donated the site; the United Nations Association of Waukesha, Wisconsin—near Kathy's home of Schofield—donated $274 for medical equipment, and the Bolivian Ministry of Public Health agreed to provide a resident physician.

It is hoped he will be able to handle the bulk of the work

when Kathy and Nancy return to the United States. Generally speaking, Peace Corps project workers seek to train their replacements from the local citizenry, rather than have new volunteers from the United States replace those whose term of service has been completed.

One of the most noteworthy Peace Corps services in Bolivia is performed by Donald Bullock of Concord, New Hampshire, and his wife Linda of Hillsborough, California. (They met and married in the Peace Corps.) With three other volunteers, they are operating a 60-patient leper colony in the tropical village of Los Negros.

Mr. Bullock is a mechanical engineer; his wife is a registered nurse. When they were sent to Bolivia early in 1962 to help improve health facilities, no one in Washington was aware of the leprosarium project. When the Bullocks heard that the American missionary organization which was running the institution was about to leave, they took over.

Relying on friends in the United States, the Bullocks were able to raise more than $2,000 in cash, plus donations of medicines and clothing, to overcome a financial crisis the institution faced. The Bolivian government contributed another $2,500, and $3,000 was raised by the New Tribes Group, a non-sectarian American missionary organization.

What one man can do in the midst of the pitiable poverty that exists in one Bolivian community is probably best exemplified by the work of a 23-year-old pharmacist from Boston named James McTigue. A Peace Corps evaluation report said he functioned like a "ward leader." In obtaining information and support, he became familiar with every power source—political, clerical, and intellectual. He became the "key to the success" of a health project in the university city of Sucre.

What did McTigue accomplish in a year's work? He set up four model wards in the university hospital and formed a nursing organization, with nurses wearing white uniforms, white stockings, and hats—something never done before. He organized three health clinics in outlying poorer areas so people could get free medicine and medical help. He got Bolivian medical students to help staff the dispensaries and began classes to educate Bolivian teachers and students to take them over.

He distributed milk to 2,000 people a day in the poor barrios outside Sucre. "We used the milk as a come on," he says, "so public health workers could get to know the people and treat them. We found babies with whooping cough and open sores. We found two broken legs."

He gave health talks over the radio. He organized doctors who speak the Indian language of Quecha so they could inform people what was available medically.

His Peace Corps assignment was not what he pictured it. "In training (at the University of Oklahoma), I dreamed about what it would be like," he says. "My dream evaporated the day I sat on a curbstone with an Indian woman who'd given birth to a baby an hour before and was about to resume her job sweeping the streets. The people didn't seem to want a health program."

After a year of work in Bolivia, McTigue requested he be allowed to leave Peace Corps service. He wanted to enter training with the Maryknoll order of priests. "I feel I grew in Bolivia. I got more understanding of the needs of other people."

By all the people, from the President of the country to

impoverished campesino, Bolivian Peace Corps volunteers are welcomed with great friendliness and enthusiasm. By all, that is, except the Communist propagandists. They branded one contingent of volunteers as "counter-guerrillas . . . mercenaries, well-trained by the U.S. Department of Defense."

An article in *Unidad,* an official Communist publication in Bolivia, said the volunteers have been instructed to use "marriage as a fighting and tactical weapon." The article points to an alleged Peace Corps stipulation that the prospective volunteer be unmarried. The unmarried volunteer, according to *Unidad,* is instructed to find and marry a host country mate for the purpose of justifying legally his or her stay in the country.

Unidad's criticism is obviously naïve. Marriage is no bar to Peace Corps service. However, married couples are only taken if they both qualify for the same project and if they have no dependent children under 18.

Unidad called the volunteers "occupation troops" and said that "they have a store of arms that would make Buck Rogers envious." It was said to include a "special weapon of lightweight arrows, powered by rockets of lethal strength and more powerful than a 30 calibre missile. It has a psychological advantage since it does not produce any noise and causes panic among those attacked," reported the article.

Such criticism is rare, however, and the Peace Corps program in Bolivia ranks as one of the organization's most successful. Since it fans out from almost all the universities and university cities of the country, its effectiveness is felt by a high percentage of the Bolivian population. The role of the university in the society of Bolivia is an important one. The only good libraries of the country are there; so are the best medical facilities. The Peace Corps, in stimulating health and community development programs through the academic institutions, and in stimulating the universities themselves into action, is performing tasks that can have a beneficial effect upon the entire population.

But it is because of its direct, people-to-people approach that the Peace Corps is most revered in Bolivia. An editorial in *La Nacion,* the official government newspaper, underscored this idea. It commented, "These Volunteers are formidable ambassadors direct from the soul and the technical side of the North American neighbors. They come in contact with the people when they arrive, and they awaken their initiative; they understand them and they leave behind them a thirst for improvement and for a better life."

Colombia

The Peace Corps program in Colombia ranks as one of the agency's largest, one of its most ambitious and one of its most complex. It was one of the Peace Corps' first programs, too. More than 600 volunteers are fanned out through the backlands of the sometimes politically-tense country, and many of them are assigned to remote villages where few United States citizens have ever set foot. (Two volunteers are stationed in Minca, a village that has no telegraph, no telephone, no mail service.)

The complexity of the Colombian program arises from its nature and the way the project is structured. Peace Corps assistance in Colombia comes under the catchall category of "Community Development." Generally, this means that volunteers take on such tasks as building roads, schools, aqueducts, and bridges. It means they may serve as health officers, training nurses, and counseling on sanitation programs. In Colombia, volunteers' work is much more diversified than these descriptions imply. According to one survey, late in 1963 there were at least 50 different types of projects in work in hundreds of different locations. Assignments in Colombia provide the volunteer with a great challenge. The volunteers have to adapt; they have to improvise. As Peace Corps officials put it, Colombia "is an exacting test of (volunteers') resourcefulness."

In a unique and extremely helpful bit of structuring, the Peace Corps program in Colombia is administered by CARE. (The Cooperative for American Relief Everywhere, Inc., CARE also assists other Peace Corps programs in Guatemala, Pakistan, and Sierra Leone.) Long-experienced in aid programs in Colombia, CARE helped to develop the training procedures for Colombia-bound volunteers and is responsible for the general administration of the project. The agency has alloted more than $100,000 for Peace Corps community action projects in the country, some of which provide volunteers with personal supplies, and part of the equipment and tools that are required. (Upon arrival in Colombia, each volunteer receives three pairs of khaki trousers, a pair of boots, and an oil burning stove.)

Another private agency, The Cooperative League of the United States, also administers a project in Colombia. A group of 25 volunteers that have been on assignment in Colombia since mid-1963; several of the men are working with handicraft cooperatives, developing ways in which domestic products can be marketed. Others are engaged in agricultural marketing.

There is a basic motive and a good one that guides all volunteer assistance projects in Colombia. The primary objective is to show the people how much they can accomplish for themselves. Volunteers are trained to stimulate action by introducing the idea of local self-reliance through democratic group action. This is a bit high-sounding, and one volunteer described programs objectives more concisely. In working with local citizens, he explained, "The idea has always been that we are to work ourselves out of a job."

In any individual program in Colombia, the first step is the organization of a village "junta," a citizens' committee. The whole concept of democratic community action is often a completely new one to the Colombian "campesino" (rural resident). One volunteer reports that some villagers have almost no knowledge of the concept of voting. Though they may occasionally cast a ballot for a national leader, voting by a show of hands and the principle of a town meeting are entirely foreign to them.

"To organize the junta, you have to do a lot of preliminary work, mostly visiting each family in the 'vereda' (village), and explaining that a good job of community action depends on a well-organized vereda," says volunteer Jim Tenaglia. "You tell them that meetings must be run in an orderly fashion, and that officers are needed to keep order and take care of the paper work and coordination.

"Then, at the first meeting of the junta, if a good representation from the community is present, you hold elections for officers, at the same time explaining that the officers are *not* the junta; rather the junta consists of every member of the community, and the officers are just the governing body and coordinators." Organizing the junta is, essentially, the most important part of each volunteer's work assignment.

The volunteer's individual success should not be determined by the number of schools or roads or health centers that are built, Jim points out. A project should be deemed successful "if the people are well-organized and can carry on projects after you leave." The volunteer in Colombia serves as a leader, though at times as a co-worker, but almost always as a catalyst toward achieving unified community action.

The physical nature of Colombia makes many Peace Corps tasks especially difficult; some are even classed as "hardship" assignments. A land mass the size of Texas and California combined, Colombia lies at the northwest corner of South America, and stretches from the Caribbean to the Pacific Ocean, across dense grasslands, tropical rain forests, and snow-topped Andean peaks. Some areas have been barely touched by civilization. In the town of Chitarque, in the State of Boyaco, no wheeled vehicles had been able to reach the village for more than five years because a bridge on an access road had collapsed. (Peace Corps volunteers, organizing local resources, got the bridge repaired.)

Most of the 14,500,000 inhabitants of the country live in the northwest section. Sixty per cent of the people are involved in agriculture. Coffee, tended, picked, and graded by hand, is the principal product.

Besides the problems presented by the physical makeup of the country, volunteers are vexed by Colombia's social ills. Poverty is rampant. The nation's per capita income is about $125 per person per year. Two per cent of the population owns 90 per cent of the wealth. Fifty per cent of the population is illiterate. In January, 1963, the country had a housing deficit of 280,000 units. Some half-a-million youngsters on a primary school level do not attend school.

The people have been raised in an atmosphere of poverty and oppression. Often volunteer projects are greeted with apathy and suspicion. "They have gotten used to their poverty and they accept it," says one volunteer.

One "promoter" (a volunteer co-worker supplied by the Colombian government) stated that, "Our campesino has lived in passiveness. He has been exploited by politicians. They have promised but haven't delivered. A grave, very grave factor is paternalism. People expect things to be given to them without making any effort. They expect them to come as manna from heaven."

But despite the problems of inertia on the part of the local citizenry, volunteers can point to any number of instances of bright success. In the words of one Peace Corps official, "Olés have been numerous."

One volunteer from Chicago, who had never planted a flower or vegetable garden in his life, has become an expert in onion growing. He found out that onions, though a popular item in the diet of Colombians, often are in short supply. So he suggested to a peasant in the area where he works that they grow onions in the peasant's field.

But the peasant protested that he had never done that, and he knew nothing about onions. Off went the volunteer to the Ministry of Agriculture in Bogota. He got literature on onions, advice from horticulturists, and the necessary seeds. At harvest time, the onion crop brought the farmer an income from his land three times greater than he had ever received before.

When one volunteer was first assigned to a small rural village, he found the Indians making decorative, useful woolen ponchos called ruanas. Merchants from Bogota came occasionally to the village, bought a few ruanas for a dollar each and then resold them in the city stores for eight dollars. Seeing an opportunity to elevate the life of the village, the volunteer had the natives improve their dyes. He organized a marketing system and convinced the natives to establish a system of quality control. Business boomed. And village income doubled, then tripled.

One volunteer was assigned to a rural Andean village where, for 500 years, the campesinos had lived within one-half-mile of good water, but it was on the other side of a mountain. Unable to persuade government officials to do anything about their situation, they simply lugged water up and down the mountain. The volunteer coaxed government officials into contributing enough pipe and cement to lay an aqueduct. The campesinos—men, women, and children—donated their labor. Active in other projects, too, the volunteer in Colombia is known as "El Hombre Que Sabe"—the Man Who Knows.

Peace Corps success can be of a more subtle variety. One volunteer recalled, "In our vereda we had organized a junta, had an election of officers, and everything started out fine. But the next time we went back to visit the vereda, the people decided the man who had been elected junta president was not doing his job. So they had a special meeting and elected new officers."

Said the volunteer: "To my way of thinking, this achieved a lot more than building a bridge or a latrine."

Volunteer Dennis Grubb, a man with 17 projects in operation in one village, says "there is no such thing as a typical day or type of schedule for how much time to spend on this or that. We have to play it by ear.

"From 8 A.M. to 6 P.M. you may be out where the people are building a school. At other times, from 8 A.M. to noon you are with the local priest, or you may spend the day with the government's Division of Community Action trying to get materials. You may spend the whole day out talking to the people in their homes, or with the president of the junta.

"Some days it takes half a day to get from one place to another to see how the work is going. When we go to a site and there is no one there, we know we have more work to do.

"If the juntas are formed well, if we can get them properly organized, help them to get aid, and get them started, we can leave them for awhile. Our job is 90 per cent relating to the people and 10 per cent doing the physical work."

Recent Peace Corps programs in Colombia have been more specialized in content. The newest volunteers have been assigned to social work in urban slums. One group, that arrived in Colombia early in 1964, attended training classes at the New York School of Social Work at Columbia University, and worked 24 hours a week in the slums of New York's lower East Side and in Harlem. In preparation for their work in Colombia, they conducted rat extermination drives and taught cooking classes. (They found some slum dwellers were throwing away such government surplus items as powdered milk because they did not know how to prepare them.)

Another recent program in Colombia is concerned with Educational Television. Involving 60 Peace Corps volunteers and an equal number of Colombian co-workers, the program, to provide basic instruction in classroom subjects, will reach 85 per cent of Colombia's population and 94 per cent of its schools.

It is difficult to appraise individual volunteer efforts in Colombia as achieving "success" or "failure." It is more difficult to evaluate whole projects in this fashion. In terms of aqueducts built, or health centers started, in terms of sports or education programs initiated, the Peace Corps effort in Colombia has never lacked for tangible results.

But in Colombia, the impact of the Peace Corps may only fully be determined when the volunteers have returned to the United States. It will depend on whether the campesino will carry on the self-help community action under a democratized system of self-government—a system the volunteer is trying to show him now.

Ethiopia

Ethiopia, Emperor Haile Selassie's independent empire in northeastern Africa, is host to one of the Peace Corps' largest and one of its most successful programs. To this country, where 90 per cent of the people are illiterate, the Peace Corps has assigned its largest contingent—276 volunteer teachers in a single project. They began service in September, 1962. (The largest Peace Corps program, in terms of volunteers, is in Colombia. There, a total of 628 volunteers work in 15 different "projects." Ethiopia boasts the largest Peace Corps "project," 276 volunteers.) The following year, a second project, involving 150 additional volunteers was assigned to the country, some as teachers, some as staff physicians and nurses, some as public health workers. All underwent training at Washington's Georgetown University.

Economically and socially, Ethiopia is in the midst of change. While more than 90 per cent of the country's 21,000,000 people are still engaged in agriculture, modernization is apparent in the form of new industrial and office buildings, and new factories and workshops. The empire is located in what is known as "The Horn of Africa," in the easternmost part of the continent below the Red Sea. The national language is Amharic, closely related to Hebrew and Arabic; English is the second language.

A country about one half again as large as the state of Texas, Ethiopia boasts a near perfect climate with a temperature range of 60 to 80 degrees throughout the year. A large part of the country is a plateau, with the average elevation about 8,000 feet. Altitude has caused some discomforts among the volunteer contingent.

So intense is the Ethiopian concern for education that the Ministry of Education is directed personally by Emperor Haile Selassie. And, as further evidence of his interest, he has donated one of his palaces for use as a university. Beulah Bartlett and Blythe Monroe, a pair of 65-year-old teacher volunteers from South Laguna, California, teach school in Dire Dawa, the hometown of Haile Selassie. One day he walked into one of Beulah's classes and sat down alongside her students. Beulah continued her class as if nothing unusual had happened. Before leaving, the Emperor congratulated Beulah. "It was the greatest moment in the history of that school," Peace Corps officials say.

The need for teachers in Ethiopia is nothing short of overpowering. Before the arrival of the Peace Corps volunteers, the country claimed a force of 476 secondary school teachers. The number supplied the needs of only 8,000 of the empire's one million children of secondary school age. With the addition of the Peace Corps instructors, another 4,000 youngsters were able to receive education. While the Peace Corps project served to improve by 50 per cent the educational standards of the country, the need for teachers and for classroom facilities remains dire.

In addition to their teaching duties, Peace Corps volunteers are engaged in a wide variety of other projects. One group is distributing grain to needy students, several groups are assembling and operating small libraries. Volunteers are participating in Ethiopian choral groups, directing dramatic productions, and setting up scouting activities.

Four volunteers in an Addis Ababa school have taken on these projects: one has organized the school's first glee club and is also coaching tennis; a second is leading a new handicraft club and is stimulating interest in a pen-friend club to correspond with American students; a third is giving music lessons and is changing the school newspaper from a two-a-year to a 13-a-year production schedule; the fourth, a woman volunteer, has organized a domestic science club and is interesting students, both boys and girls, in preparing balanced, wholesome meals.

Some volunteers have been assigned to modern schools in the bustling capital of Addis Ababa; others serve in small, remote villages where the facilities are spartan-like. Most volunteers are housed near their schools in households ranging from one to nine persons. Several groups of volunteers have invited Ethiopian students and teachers to share their homes in an effort to develop a closer relationship with their host country colleagues.

Richard Lipez, 24, of Lock Haven, Pennsylvania, is teaching at Debre Marcos, a town of 4,000 in the Province of Gojam, a region that has been isolated from the outside world since the time of Christ.

"Most of the houses are 'tukols,' round mud huts with thatched roofs," he says. "Some of the more wealthy people of the town live in square clay houses with corrugated metal roofs. A tin roof is a status symbol here," he reports.

"My first real jolt came when I was led into a hut which was the home of one of my students. A fire was burning in the center of the dirt floor, and the smoke drifted up through the grass roof. This keeps the fleas out," Dick explains. "There were two crude beds of eucalyptus branches and a collection of clay pots. This was the extent of the furnishings."

Living conditions shocked another volunteer teacher, Barbara Fountain, 24, of Denver, Colorado. "I was surprised to see children without clothes, and one day I actually had to dig flies out of a baby's eyes."

The food also presented some new experiences. Lipiz reports that the age-old dishes are "injerat," a gray sponge-like food used as bread; and the main dish, a mixture of various vegetables and hot spices called "watt." "It's a terrifying assault on one's stomach," says Lipiz. "There are no eating utensils, you simply tear off a piece of the injerat, and slop it around a bit in the common watt bowl."

Miss Fountain, a blue-eyed brunette, recalls being served a special dish made of animal intestines and stomach linings. It was said to insure that she would bear a male child.

Dick, who had never been farther than 200 miles from home before joining Peace Corps service, teaches English to 146 students in 26 periods of instruction each week. "Communication between teachers and students falters at times," he states, "but we are intent on getting through and the students want desperately to learn. Some of them walk from isolated villages hundreds of miles over mountains and plains to reach school."

Dick says, "The simplified edition of *Lamb's Tales from Shakespeare* is the most popular prose. The students are fascinated by the bloody struggle for power among the Scottish nobility in *Macbeth*. The students like to soar lumpily along with Tennyson, although Robert Frost is easily the most popular poet. His simplicity of language and tales of country things go down well."

In response to a flood of pleas from book-starved volunteers, the Peace Corps now ships to each person on overseas assignment a $70 portable paperback library packed in a rugged storage locker, paid for out of Peace Corps funds. The library is made up of about 175 books covering historical, social, and economic aspects of American life. There's a good amount of representative American fiction in the library, too. The library includes Saroyan's *Human Comedy* (in Urdu, if the volunteer wants), Lewis' *Dodsworth* (available in Bengali), and Dr. Spock's *Baby and Child Care* (in almost every language). Among the authors represented are Twain, Cooper, Hawthorne, James, Crane,

Wolfe, Wilder, Tocqueville, Lord Bryce, Harry Truman, and Erle Stanley Gardner. Gene Rosaschi and Jerry Lemert, a pair of volunteers from Glide, Oregon, who are serving as teachers in Dessie, Ethiopia, cataloged their supply of books and set up a lending library. "You can't imagine how hungry these students are to read anything and everything," Gene says. "The teachers have a library at school, but the students aren't allowed to use it. And there are no libraries or bookstores in Dessie at all."

To almost all of the volunteers, the students seem terribly eager to learn. "They are very curious about America, too," says William Mihay of Centerville, Indiana, teaching with seven other volunteers in Yirga Alem, a town of 14,000 people. "They ask about discrimination against colored people frequently.

"The students call us 'Sir.' Even the soldiers salute us. When the teacher walks into a room, the entire class comes to attention, and sits down only when the teacher has acknowledged them with a slight bow. All students stand up to recite and speak only when they are standing."

Sally Timmel, along with 13 volunteer companions, teaches in the only secondary school in Makale, the capital of Tigre province. She and the other volunteers are the only white people in the city. They are the subject of great curiosity; children stare at them.

She spends some of her off hours tending to a small garden that consists of some stunted sweet corn, squash, peas, and radishes. Evenings are spent grading papers, mimeographing notes, correcting tests, or, sometimes, entertaining foreign visitors who pass through Makale. Once every few weeks, she treks north to Asmara to buy food supplies for the household. Other weekends, picnics are planned.

"Our teaching day is normal as any other around the world," Sally says. "I teach six sections of ninth grade science to about 250 students, most of them boys, between 15 and 21."

In their everyday work assignments, the Ethiopian students quaintly demonstrate the great disparity between their language and culture and ours. One student, in submitting a simple declarative sentence, used the example, "She wears glass on her ears and many cloths." Another student conjugated the word lack, "Lack, lick, luck."

In a country where the role of the woman has traditionally been one of subservience, the acceptance of women as teachers has been mixed. Older staff members, particularly, have been slow to take to the idea of women instructors. One bright young girl, fresh from volunteer training, arrived in Addis Ababa to be told she had four distinct disadvantages; first, she was new; second, she was young; third, she was a woman; fourth, she was attractive. For many girl volunteer teachers, adaptability is a prime talent.

It cannot be denied that the Peace Corps volunteers in Ethiopia have been responsible for an important step forward in Ethiopian education. When regarded in the light of the grave educational problems facing the country, their contribution may seem slight, yet the Peace Corps has made possible the largest single increase in the number of people educated in Ethiopian public schools since the school system was established in 1908.

A further good established by the Peace Corps contingent is evidenced by the fact that the Ethiopians are expressing interest in establishing an Ethiopian counterpart to work with, and later, carry on the programs of the volunteers. And the further hope is that these Ethiopian educators either alone, or with American volunteers, will go into the provinces—heretofore educationally untouched —to teach and help develop these remote areas.

Nigeria

Pretty Bertha Evosevich, from Pittsburgh, was the only school teacher in the only school in the small town of Owo in the western region of Nigeria. One day, late in 1963, Bertha had to tell her students that her two-year stay as a Peace Corps volunteer had ended; she was going home to America.

"Madame, you can't do that," one of her little girls insisted. "We love you so much."

Some other pupils had a solution. Why, they asked, didn't she marry one of their fathers. She could be a third or fourth wife—and she would be their mother.

Miss Evosevich compromised; she became a godmother to one of the girls.

For the more than 300 Peace Corps volunteers in Nigeria, teaching is a daily drama. Nigeria has 40 million inhabitants, and all of them black; no white settlers live there. And in all of Nigeria, there are only 1,700 degree-holding teachers.

The Peace Corps program in Nigeria is a high calibre one. The training courses are among the best offered by the agency with such seats of learning as Columbia University, Harvard, and Michigan State providing the educators and educational facilities. To head the Nigerian program, Sargent Shriver chose William G. Saltonstall, since 1945, principal of Phillips Exeter Academy, in Exeter, New Hampshire. Prior to taking up his position in Nigeria, in June, 1963, Mr. Saltonstall had been president of the New England Association of Colleges and Secondary Schools, and a member of the executive committee of the American Council on Education. It is rumored he is slated to be Sargent Shriver's successor as Peace Corps Director.

Teachers College at Columbia University has trained more than 400 Peace Corps volunteers for African assignments, mainly in teaching, and mainly for Nigeria. Columbia's training programs are ones of excellence, their pre-eminence doubtlessly due to the long-standing interest of Teachers College in international education, particularly African education. Columbia's interest dates to before World War II when African students first began courses of instruction at Teachers College.

In July, 1960—a full year before the Peace Corps was active—the Afro-Anglo-American Program in Teacher Education was created with headquarters at Columbia's Teachers College. Teamed with the Institute of Education at the University of London and nine universities and university colleges in Africa, Columbia launched an exchange teacher training program. In addition, Columbia's Teachers College has administered a "Teachers for East Africa" Program, supported by AID funds, since early 1961.

In knowledge and experience, in its teaching personnel,

Teachers College was enviably equipped when it took on the training of Peace Corps volunteers for Sierra Leone in the fall of 1961. A year later, Teachers College trained the first of several Nigerian Peace Corps contingents.

Nigeria, the size of Oklahoma and Texas combined, lies along the Guinea Coast of Africa, once called the white man's graveyard. From this part of Africa came the forebears of American slaves. In climate, Nigeria conforms to the American concept of Africa: much of the country is dense coastal jungle; heat and humidity almost overwhelm the American.

By 1972, the Government of Nigeria hopes to have a total of 85,000 professionally and technically trained Nigerians. But the country today has only 7,000 qualified teachers and only 1,700 of these hold degrees. Peace Corps teachers are represented in 15 per cent of the nation's schools and they also make up 15 per cent of the graduate teaching supply.

Some volunteers are surprised by what they do not find in Nigeria. Alan Margolis returned to his Brooklyn home after completing two years of teaching service in the Nigerian town of Ife, a city of 150,000 in the southwestern part of the country. His friends in Brooklyn question him about lions, big game hunts, picturesque native huts, and bullock carts. Mr. Margolis explains that the people of Ife haven't seen lions for 25 years. "Most of the people live in stone or mud houses, not huts, on stilts with thatched roofs. As for transportation, most people either use cars or bicycles."

Some volunteers instruct at schools located in the remote bush. It is not easy. "Teaching school can be a 24-hour-a-day job," one teacher says. "There is no water in our school building except that which we bring in buckets. There are Bunsen burners which operate from a portable cylinder. We have some balances, a fair supply of chemicals, a blackboard, plenty of chalk, and that's about it."

The lack of teaching supplies is often compensated for by the eagnerness to learn on the part of the Nigerian youngsters. "When they are given extra work to do, they do it and love it," remarked a returning volunteer teacher. "And they are much better disciplined than American pupils. They automatically rise and come to attention when the teacher walks into the classroom."

Many volunteers have been assigned to teaching and research positions at the University of Nigeria at Nsukka, in the Eastern provinces of the country. In March, 1960, the university was no more than an idea. But since that time, 20 concrete classroom buildings and dormitories to serve more than a thousand students have been built and others are under construction. For construction of the university, the Eastern Provinces of Nigeria are spending more than $14 million, money that was received from the sale of palm oil. A fair-sized city is springing up in what was once a wide stretch of bush and yam patches.

During the rainy season, the hills around the university are covered with long, wavy green grass. When the dry season begins, the grass is burned to make way for new growth and the hills stand black and stark. Volunteer teachers never cease to marvel at the strange and natural beauty of the terrain.

The typical university student in Nigeria is unlike his American counterpart. He is older; the average age is 28. He is married. He is always serious and hard-working. Before becoming a student, he was most likely a secondary school teacher. He is intensely interested in world affairs, and he wants to enter law, diplomacy, or civil service after completing his university training. The chances are good that he will become a leader of his country.

Late in November, 1961, a group of 23 Peace Corps volunteers arrived in Nsukka, ready for teaching and research assignments at the university. They had had intensive training at Michigan State University in a program administered by the university's extremely capable African studies staff. On arrival in Nigeria, they were welcomed by the Prime Minister, Sir Abubakar Balewa, and by other officials of the Nigerian and other African governments. In the coastal city of Lagos, they received four days of orientation, and then they left on a two-day, 500-mile bus ride, through the bush, through the rain forests, over the savannahs, and across the Niger River to Nsukka. But their greeting at the university was less than enthusiastic. There was a feeling of distrust and even suspicion toward the Americans. Much of this was due to the furore created by the greatly-publicized "Michelmore incident."

Margery Michelmore was a 23-year-old school teacher from Massachusetts who, with 24 other volunteers, was undergoing in-country training in Nigeria. Like most all of the trainees, she found living conditions in Ibadan, as in most all of Nigeria, so primitive as to shock. The great majority of Nigerians live according to the tribal ways of their ancestors; their habits have gone unchanged for centuries.

On a post card to a friend in the United States, Miss Michelmore wrote, "With all the training we had had, we were really not prepared for the squalor and the absolutely primitive living conditions . . . Everyone except us lives in the streets, cooks in the streets, and even goes to the bathroom in the streets."

Miss Michelmore's succinct report never got to her friend in the United States. She lost it on the campus, and it was recovered by a Nigerian student. Within two hours, the post card had been duplicated and copies were distributed throughout the university to the volatile Nigerian students. (Three times, in 1961, they had taken part in anti-American demonstrations.) Copies of the post card were furnished to the local press who rose to a virulent attack on Miss Michelmore. One paper called for her to be deported.

The Nigerian government came to the Peace Corps' defense (though they hinted Miss Michelmore should be returned home), but a group of students, demonstrating on the Ibadan campus, called for the expulsion of the entire Peace Corps contingent. Some of the faculty joined in the anti-American outburst. In some quarters, the whole incident was put into a racial context, and the post card was cited as being typical of the contempt American whites felt for African blacks.

The speed with which the anti–Peace Corps demonstrations were organized is probably an indication that some students were waiting for an opportunity of the type Miss Michelmore presented to attack the Peace Corps. Unfortunately, the effects of the incident were not limited to the campus at Ibadan. The story of the rally was carried around the world. Many press accounts—principally the local ones—claimed a thousand students had attended the protest rally; Peace Corps officials say that only 150 to 200 students were in attendance.

Miss Michelmore's indiscretion came to be the most serious of all the Peace Corps growing pains. She was returned to the United States. Congress charged that the event showed the inadequacy of Peace Corps training. But, in the long range, the incident probably achieved more good than harm. For it showed the Peace Corps volunteer, no matter where he was serving, the very sensitive nature of his status and the great vulnerability of his position. In this regard, the ill-fated post card accomplished more than a score of memos from Washington headquarters.

The day-to-day work of the Peace Corps volunteer in Nigeria has overcome the ill-feeling that existed in 1961. The aforementioned group of 23 volunteers at the University of Nigeria has completed its work. They lectured in history, sociology, political science, English, economics, and music. They assisted in sociological studies of surrounding villages. They taught secretarial courses and office management courses. They helped the local district officer perform a census. They conducted night classes for the university's junior staff. The volunteers did their jobs well. As their tour of duty neared its close late in 1963, *The Nsukka Record,* the student newspaper at the university, said, "We feel that no amount of praise showered on them for their work is too much."

Volunteers, whether teaching in the new universities of the country, or in the scattered secondary schools, find that once the attitude toward newness wears off, boredom can become a problem. The job settles into a routine. Opportunities for diversion are few. Most areas are without movie theaters or even stores. "Despite all the glamorous talk and publicity, we have a perfectly straightforward job to do here," said one volunteer. "We're teachers—just as we would be at schools anywhere." Preparing lectures, holding student conferences, and correcting papers falls into a regular pattern.

The restlessness that some volunteers experience is increased by school vacations. Some universities close for three or four months during the summer. In western Nigeria, secondary schools shut down for seven weeks in August and September.

To many volunteers, such breaks in the teaching routine are opportunities to conduct research or plan scientific studies in the Nigerian hinterland. One volunteer, during a school hiatus, is working on the first written vocabulary and grammar of a remote tribal language of the north country. Another joined a university expedition of the Institute of African Studies and traveled on a historical research project through the northern stretches of the country. Other volunteers worked with the United Nations Food and Agricultural Organization on an irrigation survey.

Other "off-time" projects are more scholastic in nature. Some volunteers set to work simply rewriting school syllabus material. Some organize school or town libraries. Some fill in as teachers in other areas where different school schedules are in effect. During school vacations, volunteers have constructed dispensaries, they have built chemistry laboratories; they have instituted day camps and community centers. Fifteen volunteers teaching at the University of Nigeria spent a vacation building a steel and cement water tower for the village of Ugbaike, and local volunteers worked side-by-side with the Peace Corps.

"Send us more Peace Corps workers," say government officials in Nigeria. And the Peace Corps is responding. Altogether, more than 500 volunteers have trained for service in Nigeria and more projects are in the planning or training stage. Almost 200 volunteers have completed service in Nigeria and have returned to the United States. In terms of the number of volunteers, the Nigerian program is the largest in Africa.

In helping the Nigerian government to expand secondary and higher education, the Peace Corps program has provided substantial assistance. In terms of host country impact and total contribution, the Nigerian teaching project is one of the Peace Corps' most successful. But Peace Corps programs invariably have secondary effects. As one volunteer said, "The Peace Corps has done as much or more good for its volunteers than it has for other countries."

One of the great impediments to the success of the Peace Corps service in Nigeria, or in any Negro country, for that matter, are the indignities experienced by Nigerian officials who serve in the United States. Paul Conklin, writing in *The New Republic* said, "to the Nigerian mind, a cup of coffee denied outweighs all the good that American missionaries, doctors, nurses, teachers, and aid technicians are performing throughout the country—and the same cup of coffee counts for more than a score of nuclear tests in the Soviet Union."

If the returning Peace Corps volunteers, through their two-year broadening experience, can increase appreciation for the people and countries of Africa in their own country, then, on this score alone, their service will have been worthwhile.

Pakistan

In Pakistan, the Peace Corps is nation-building. More than 250 volunteers serve in the East and West wings of the country in a wide assortment of tasks. They assist in public works programs, building schools, irrigation works, roads, and small bridges; they help to promote agriculture production. There are 11 volunteer nurses in the country; there are 35 volunteer teachers. The needs in Pakistan are overpowering: 95 per cent of the country's 100,000,000 people (it is the sixth largest nation in the world) live in poverty.

East and West Pakistan are split into two parts by 1,200 miles of Indian territory, and they show marked differences in culture, language, terrain, and climate. The West wing of the country, with a population of 45,000,000 people, is the size of Texas and Louisiana combined, and six times larger than the East section. Urdu is the principal language, although English is common among students. (Pakistani students have difficulty understanding the American accent in contrast to the British accent to which they are accustomed.)

In the West, volunteers serve in the ancient bazaar city of Peshawar and in the renowned desert city of Hyderabad. They become familiar with the mud of the monsoon seasons and the dust at every other time of the year. Towns and villages are constructed largely of mud and cow dung, and the black and white dress of the villagers contrasts sharply with the Oriental-influenced East Pakistanis.

Volunteers bound for the East section of Pakistan are schooled in the Bengali language. In the East, the country is flat with low-lying valleys. Volunteers experience hot summers and cool winters and the torrential monsoon rains of June through August that seem to completely engulf the land. Fifty-five million people live in East Pakistan.

In both East and West, the ancient Muslim call to prayers is heard from the top of every mosque five times a day. It was, in fact, because of its religious proclivities that Pakistan was founded. In 1947, when the British withdrew from India, the country split along religious lines, with Muslim oriented sections becoming what is known as Pakistan and the Hindu-controlled areas becoming the Union of India. Today, Pakistan ranks as the largest Muslim country in the world.

Old and established patterns of society continue to prevail in all sections of the country. Women have a completely subordinate status and many villages still observe "purdah," the traditional segregation of women and men from life outside the home. Purdah also means that, in a public place, a woman must cover her head and face with a veil. Some women, for their entire lifetime, never emerge from the village compound. One volunteer nurse noted that some women have never seen a doctor, and, only after a long discussion with one such sick woman and her husband, could she get the woman to a local hospital.

Another nurse volunteer, Regina Ruhl of Seattle, Washington, who supervises the nursing staff at a backwoods maternity hospital, has to hold periodic roll calls, "because the patients have been known to flee en masse, if a man enters the ward."

Another annoyance is locks. "Everything—but everything—is padlocked," she says. "The more important the objects being hidden, the bigger the lock. Opening and closing these locks takes up a good share of the nurse's time during the day."

The customs not only present Nurse Ruhl with problems; so does the equipment scarcity. For a 50 bed hospital, she has only two thermometers and two syringes. "We have to juggle duties and schedules in order to use the equipment correctly and yet maintain some routine in the work."

Like most developing countries where the Peace Corps serves, Pakistan needs urgent help in agriculture. Although blessed with a fertile soil and an adequate water supply, the productivity of the land is among the world's lowest. In some areas, during an average five-year period, a farmer will have one good year, one bad year, and three years in which he is barely able to eke out subsistence for himself and his family.

Two volunteers, Ray Duff, 22, of Pendleton, Oregon, and Dave Morris, a 20-year-old farmer from Perryton, Texas, have been working as agricultural engineers in Khanewal, a farming center of about 30,000 people in West Pakistan. Before the arrival of the volunteers, the villages in the area had purchased 65 tractors and were using them on a co-operative basis. But the government-sponsored project never took into account that the tractors would require preventive maintenance and repair. As a result, when the tractors broke down, they were cast aside; they stood idle.

Despite a lack of spare parts, tools, and trained mechanics, the two volunteers are setting up a network of repair shops in the farm villages. Their goal is a profound one: to restore the farmer's faith in agricultural mechanization. When Duff first arrived on the scene, he recalled he was skeptical as to the practicality of farm mechanization in the area. "You could see so many tractors lying around unused because of lack of spare parts, and I didn't see how things could be any different. But the people are conscientious and making the project a success. . . ."

Morris reported that, "Our major accomplishment so far has been winning their confidence. When we first came, they looked us over real closely. But now they trust us." He continued, "Recently, they gave us 4,000 rupees in cash (about $1,000), a tremendous sum for them, and told us to buy what we felt was necessary."

The farm land around Khanewal is slowly being reclaimed from the desert. Water exists in the area in ample quantities below the surface of the ground. So, in addition to the tractor maintenance program, Duff and Morris are also assisting in an extensive well-digging scheme. Under the plan, each village will buy pumps co-operatively until each village has two.

In West Pakistan, other agriculturally-trained volunteers are at work conducting experiments using commercial fertilizer on gardens and fruit trees. Often, simple bits of information are especially valuable. One volunteer found a village where garden peas took six months to mature, grew to a six-foot height, and were heavy with foliage but skimpy with peas. He simply introduced villagers to a method of staking the pea vines and encouraged planting them in a compact area.

The social customs of the country sometimes present the

volunteer with unique and frustrating problems. For instance, an educated Pakistani seldom works with his hands. "For a person of intelligence to stoop and pick up a piece of clay or a wrench or demonstrate the use of a wheel-barrow or steel hoes would be impossible," says one volunteer. The educated person feels that he is superior to people who must touch dirt or lift loads.

At Kotpindas, a village outside Lahore, in West Pakistan, James McKay, a volunteer from Hornell, New York, organized some of his fellow Peace Corps workers and some Pakistani friends to repair a 300-year-old Mongol bridge. It took some convincing because the middle-class Pakistanis had never used shovels. A group of villagers came by and asked, "What, no peasants?" Then, seeing the "sahibs" hard at work, pitched in, too.

Volunteer teachers in Pakistan are also confronted with difficult situations arising from the social makeup of the country. (There are about 40 Peace Corps teachers in Pakistan, most of them instructing in the sciences.) Most often these problems are encountered in major cities and at higher academic levels. Students are much more politically conscious than in the United States, and student strikes are an accepted part of academic life. And, in a carry-over from the British educational system, emphasis is on the rote method of learning.

Conrad Linkiewicz, 31, of New Bedford, Massachusetts, taught a course in "Industrial Arts Woodwork" at the Dacca (East Pakistan) Polytechnic Institute. He was one of the first volunteers in the country, taking up his assignment in October, 1961.

Now returned to the United States, Mr. Linkiewicz recalls that his workshop was outfitted "with a very adequate supply of every type of woodworking machine." They were provided through a Ford Foundation grant. "The only problem," he says, "was an adequate supply of parts and accessories." As in the case of the tractors of the Khanewal farm country, many machines sat idle for lack of parts.

Mr. Linkiewicz reports that his superiors at the school directed him to "follow the course outline which has been followed for the last few years." It called for the students to make joints which had no practical use at all. The corners of Mr. Linkiewicz' workshop were piled high with hundreds of joints that previous classes had made.

Mr. Linkiewicz did not attempt to make skilled carpenters or cabinet makers of the Pakistani youths. Instead, he tried to get them to think, to reason, and make decisions for themselves. "Too many of them," he says, in a holdover from British educational policies, "were too dependent on the teacher and continually used him as a crutch."

Pakistan is a vast country, with a population half that of the United States, and an attempt to assess the Peace Corps program in the country is a near impossibility. As Kingston Berlew, Peace Corps Representative for Pakistan, expresses it, "The burdens and accomplishment of the volunteers cannot be measured by a recital of individual successes or even individual difficulties."

Perhaps, though, the work of the program in Pakistan can be judged from the words of a Pakistani university official who commented, "I expected two things from the Peace Corps—job competence and dedication. They have them both. I love them."

The Philippines

Scattered through the islands of the Philippines, the Peace Corps maintains a vast teaching program using the talents of more than 600 volunteers. In its early stages, it was—from the standpoint of the volunteers themselves—the most criticized of all programs. But Peace Corps/Philippines has come to be one of the most highly honored of all the agency's programs. And it also stands as one of the most significant of the entire Peace Corps movement.

One of the very first Peace Corps programs, its beginnings go back to October, 1961, when 128 volunteers were dispatched from the United States for Philippine assignment. During the next 15 months, eight additional groups followed. From the beginning, the program in the Philippines was set to be an "impact" project—it set an important national goal for itself, that of improving the quality of the Philippine public school system, especially in the remote areas of the archipelago. It is achieving its goal nicely.

Today, volunteers are at work in close to 400 rural elementary schools, some living in near primitive "barrios" (villages); some are more than 12 hours by bus or boat from the nearest Peace Corps household. They help to teach the English language, and also science, mathematics, and other subjects.

Although educational instruction is the prime motive of the program, the Peace Corps volunteer in the Philippines has an extremely active role in barrio life. Here, more than in any other country, volunteers conform to the standard American image of Peace Corps life. Volunteers live in thatch roof houses with the barest facilities. They eat and drink the food of the Filipinos; they sleep on hard beds or mats under mosquito nets; they wade through mud to go to schools. They are exposed daily to amoebas and active tuberculosis.

Although the first volunteers felt a general enthusiasm toward their work, there were occasional disillusionments in assigned responsibilities. Some were shocked by the extent of poverty that existed, but the major frustrations— in the early days of the Philippine project, at least—were brought on by a lack of definition in assignments. Though volunteers were assigned to teaching tasks, they were not considered, nor were they allowed to act as, qualified teachers. They were to serve as "educational sides," a job position which previously had not existed and which lacked clear definition.

Filipino educators were among the first to request Peace Corps volunteers from the United States, and they asked for more than a thousand volunteers to work in barrio schools and assist in English comprehension and pronunciation. (Beginning with the time the Philippines gained their independence in 1953, speaking and writing of English showed a marked downward trend. The Peace Corps program was planned to overcome this failing.) But the teachers requested by the Philippine educational authorities were not permitted to "teach"—in the fear that they would supplant and take jobs away from Filipino instructors. Hence, the role of "sides" was hit upon.

Some volunteers found the role of educational side to be so vague as to be meaningless. Some sat in the back of their classroom for the first three months waiting for the principal to tell them something to do. Other volunteers took advantage of the flexibility their assignment offered. They turned to community development work, or they helped to introduce second-language teaching methods in English, mathematics, and science. Early in 1963, however, the policies that governed the assignment of Peace Corps volunteers were revised. The job and term "educational side" was dropped, and a program was introduced that more thoroughly integrated the Peace Corps volunteer into the Philippine educational system.

Another growing pain in the Philippines was the language. Somehow, at first, the misconception prevailed that all Filipinos spoke English, and that there was no necessity for volunteers to learn one or more of the 80-odd Filipino dialects. But an official representative of the Peace Corps in the Philippines quickly became aware that language training was a "must," if the volunteer was to develop a warm and basic contact with the people of the barrio. Volunteers of recent projects have been dialect-trained at the University of Hawaii.

One early group of volunteers spent weeks learning Tagalog, the Philippine national language. But the group was assigned to non-Tagalog speaking areas. Mistakes of this type led to a complete Philippine language codification program carried out by the volunteers. Today, courses in the six basic dialects of the country are given at the Central Philippine University and the Philippine Center for Language Study.

Another problem, much more profound and much more vexing, has hampered the effectiveness of the Philippine volunteer. As expressed by Dr. Lawrence Fuchs, former

Dean of Faculty at Brandeis University and, until May, 1963, Peace Corps Representative in the Philippines, the problem involves "the fundamental indifference which has been part of the Malayan culture for centuries." Says Dr. Fuchs, volunteer efforts can be stifled by "a remarkably deep resistance of rural Filipinos to certain fundamental qualities of American life: belief in progress, confidence in science, individualism, and faith in education."

Apathy and indifference have been a constant source of volunteer frustration. "No one expected the work we did to take so much time. We got to our village and found the people didn't care," said one volunteer. "Americans have to go, go, go; but the Filipino has no concept of time. He wants to do things next week, and next week never comes."

Dr. Fuchs says that, "You think the people are burning to have you teach them English, science, and mathematics. You find they are delighted to have you," says Dr. Fuchs, "but not for these things."

Because of these problems, tangible results of the teaching programs, in some areas, are difficult to perceive. However, the Peace Corps volunteers have won universal acceptance and appreciation on the part of the barrio citizen. Nowhere do Peace Corps volunteers live as deeply and as intimately with the local citizenry as they do in the Philippines.

Volunteers are usally assigned to towns of 10,000 to 15,000 in population. Philippine municipalities consist of many barrios, the largest of which, the "poblacion," is the seat of the local government. Volunteers usually live in the poblacion, and one of the volunteers teaches in the poblacion's central school while the other instructs in one or more of the barrio schools. Most often, the volunteers live in teams of two in houses that they rent, although in some communities houses have been constructed especially for volunteers. They are of open-frame, wood construction with nipa (palm) or cogon (grass) roofs. In some of the cooler mountain areas, houses may have glass windows or corrugated metal roofs.

In Philippine houses, running water is rare. So are flush toilets. So is electricity. If a community does have electrical power, it is probably available only in the early evening. Since refrigeration is virtually non-existent, and since ice is not always available, marketing is a daily necessity. Fish and rice are diet basics. Beef is rarely seen. Pork is fairly common. Cooking facilities are primitive.

Many Peace Corps teachers have been supplied with bicycles and some have jeeps. Often they are of extreme value in remote areas. Volunteer Dick Gilbert received an emergency call one night to rush a woman who was having a baby to the hospital. The jeep, one that had been parachuted into the islands during the war, broke down on the way. The baby was born on the back seat, and by the thoughtful parents was named "Jeep Gilbert Ragay."

American-produced motion pictures, combined with the Filipino belief in the double standard, have created a sharp social problem for volunteers. Among Filipinos, there exists the widespread impression that Americans are creatures of terribly easy virtue. When men volunteers seek to date Filipino girls, their intentions are highly suspect.

Girl volunteers find the problem much more severe than do the men. Though the annoyances suffered by the girls are largely verbal, some have had to physically fend off potential molesters. "Some of the young men expected me to act like the girl in 'Butterfield 8,' " said one demure fe-male volunteer.

Generally speaking, and it is especially true in the re-mote regions of the country, girls among the volunteer con-tingent stay at home after sundown. Seldom, if ever, do they roam about unprotected. This restrictiveness has somewhat served to hamper the girls' effectiveness as volun-teers in that it limits the people-to-people aspect of their activity.

As in most countries where they serve, volunteers, al-most without exception, have been quizzed on the prob-lems of race relations in the United States. One American Negro girl silenced critics by telling them she has en-countered more difficulties in the Philippines because of her race than she ever had in her home state of Oregon.

In the Philippines today, more than 500 volunteers are working in elementary schools. Many of them teach Eng-lish, many science. While the Philippines—for decades—have built schools and trained teachers, there is a funda-mental lack in their educational system. Among Peace Corps officials, it is felt there has been a deficiency in stress-ing the "how" of learning. Students learn by rote; they memorize. It is difficult for them to be creative or to ex-press themselves effectively in English. This is a situation faced constantly on the elementary school level.

Seventy volunteers are at work in higher education, help-ing to revise and expand high school mathematics and science courses, in a number of test schools. Forty others work in universities or normal schools on remedial English and English education projects.

The contribution of the large contingent of Peace Corps volunteers in the Philippines is a growing one. Learning from the problems and the frustrations of earlier projects, recent Philippine-based programs produce results that are more readily apparent and more concrete. Dr. Fuchs says that volunteers searchingly question their own motives and the efficacy of the Peace Corps in helping the Philippines. "They feel," he says, "they are taking and learning much more than they can possibly give or teach." Certainly, this feeling is one of very positive results.

Early in 1963, President Macapagal of the Philippines presented to the "Peace Corps in Asia" the Ramon Magsaysay Award for International Understanding. It is hailed as Asia's equivalent to the Nobel Prize. The Peace Corps is the first group of Americans ever to receive the prize.

According to Sargent Shriver, the award committee privately and thoroughly checked out nominations in each country by conducting quiet and diligent surveys to see if the people at the "grass roots" level concurred in the official nomination. And the committee selection was borne out by a consensus of Asian people in countries where the Peace Corps is at work. The Magsaysay Award served to underscore the value that the average Filipino places on the day-by-day, people-to-people, effort of the Peace Corps volunteer. More than English-fluent Filipinos, this deep-seated friendship for, and basic understanding of, the American citizen may yet be the greatest benefit to come from Peace Corps work in the Philippines.

St. Lucia

Tiny St. Lucia, one of the group of Windward Islands strewn between such meccas of tourism as the Virgin Islands and Trinidad, boasts stately palm trees, bright sandy beaches, and a sparkling sea. But few tourists visit the island. There is no glamour; there is little appeal. For St. Lucia has a hundred-year history of poverty and malnutrition.

Like Colombia, Tanganyika, and Ghana, the St. Lucian Peace Corps project was one of the agency's very first. Late in the 1950's, before the American Peace Corps program had become a reality, the government of St. Lucia had already launched its own educational and health programs to encourage better techniques of animal raising, food production and preparation, child care and personal hygiene. But the St. Lucian government was seriously handicapped by a shortage of trained personnel. So with the announcement of the American Peace Corps in 1961, the government of St. Lucia saw the opportunity to obtain a volunteer contingent which could supplement local manpower resources on the island.

Foreign governments obtain Peace Corps assistance by asking for it. Requests from foreign countries for Peace Corps volunteers are often directed to the American ambassador in the foreign country; sometimes, as in the case of St. Lucia, the Peace Corps assignment is tied in with a mission of the Agency for International Development.

St. Lucia has a population of just over 100,000 people. Working among them are 15 Peace Corps volunteers, one of the agency's smallest projects.

Arable land is scarce on this small island. (It measures only 27 miles in length and 14 miles in width.) The average farmer must scratch out a living on less than four acres. Much of the soil that is worked is wasted; farmers, for generations, have used the soil until it becomes exhausted, and then moved on to a new area. Erosion is a grave problem, too. The torrential tropical rains strip the hillsides of topsoil.

Soil conservation is a main area of Peace Corps work. But volunteers in this small contingent also have assignments in teaching, teacher-training, public health education, and they also organize and work with rural youth groups.

Living conditions for the volunteers do not begin to approach the opulence of the luxury hotels a few hundred miles to the north. Some Peace Corps workers are housed in a former British army barracks in the chief city of the island, Castries. (St. Lucia is a British possession.) Built in the 1870's, it is solid, and, according to one volunteer, "monstrous." It does have electricity—at least one bulb in each room. It has a kitchen; and a washing machine that, to the delight of volunteers, "heats its own water."

In mid-October, 1961, soon after the first group of volunteers arrived to work on St. Lucia, a typhoid epidemic broke out in the southern half of the island. Some of the volunteers immediately became involved in a health project designed to stamp out the disease. They helped to install latrines, to give inoculations, and they helped in conducting a crash health education program.

In addition to the serious health problem that confronted the first volunteers, they found a problem in handling the island patois. They had anticipated no difficulty in this area for English is the official language of the island and spoken in all of the towns, but in the back country, a variety of French is spoken that is difficult to learn. In the dialect of the backwoods, volunteers are hailed as members of the "Pisco" or the "Peace Cop" or even the "Peace Corks."

The Peace Corps program in St. Lucia is administered jointly by the Peace Corps and the Heifer Project, Inc., an inter-faith, non-profit organization that sends livestock and poultry to under-developed countries. Completely philanthropic in makeup, the Heifer program's one stipulation is that recipients of the stock give the first offspring to a deserving neighbor.

In January, 1962, 25 geese, donated by a Maryland hatchery, were dispatched to St. Lucia by Heifer, along with a supply of incubators. The geese were divided up among three schools on the island, and they began laying eggs immediately.

Melin Skretvedt, of Gary, Minnesota, is the volunteer in charge of this particular project and he reports that the geese will lay up to 60 eggs a year, and if "all eggs are kept for hatching and all females for breeding purposes, in a few years time the original 25 will have increased to thousands." The geese also are meant to increase the food supply on the island and, being good grazers, are used to keep down weeds on the banana plantations. Breeding and raising programs involving Heifer-provided hogs and chickens are under way on the island, too.

Sugar was St. Lucia's chief export for centuries, but with

the abolishment of slavery in the 19th century, the once thriving large plantations went into a slow economic collapse. Today, bananas are the principal agricultural product. However, they are a fragile crop, easily destroyed by lashing, tropical storms. Bananas are also a luxury product, the American housewife will pass them by when there is a pinch in her food budget.

Peace Corps volunteers seek to help farmers diversify their crops. Coffee, avocados, and citrus crops are being introduced to the island. But the farmers are conservative in nature and slow to accept change.

Bill Hundley, 24, of Cle Elum, Washington, one of the original volunteers assigned to the island, recalls that the farmers have the wasteful practice of burning all of the fallen trees and branches from newly-cleared farm acreage. Bill tried to get them to use this "slash" as compost. He recalls this conversation with a back country farmer.

"You know if you let this slash lie on the ground, it will rot quickly and make plenty of good food for the soil."

"Yes, sir," the farmer replied.

"You know if you burn it you will lose a lot?"

"Yes, sir."

"Are you going to burn?"

"Yes, sir."

A shortage of trained teachers hampers the Peace Corps' education program on St. Lucia. Only 5 per cent of the island's elementary school teachers had a high school education. The Peace Corps supplies home economics teachers; agricultural teachers to work with primary school boys and industrial arts teachers.

In numbers of volunteers, the St. Lucia Peace Corps program is one of the agency's smallest, yet it has compiled

an impressive list of accomplishments. Because of the relatively small area covered by the project, and because of the
small population of the country, it is not unlikely that the
work of the volunteers will touch the lives of all of the St.
Lucians, demonstrating to them that a skilled utilization
of human and technical resources can make a better life
possible.

Tanganyika

The 35 Peace Corps volunteers who completed training for
a combination engineer-surveyor-geologist program in
Tanganyika, at Texas Western College in El Paso, in
August, 1961, were a much celebrated group. A good professional contingent, they were the very first volunteers to
enter training and as such they were showcased to the
nation and, in fact, to the world. After training at Texas
Western and their first dose of Swahili, they were flown to
Washington to meet President Kennedy, and then on to
New York to visit the United Nations and Adlai Stevenson.
    Then, after a month of training as "outward bounders"
at Arecibo, the Peace Corps' Puerto Rico Training Center,
they were dispatched by plane to the Tanganyika School
of Natural Resources, at Tengeru, on the slopes of Mount
Kilimanjaro for another eight weeks of instruction. Here,

in a hot, mosquito-filled classroom, the awakening took place.

"Who will we be training here?" a volunteer asked the English highway engineer who presided. When the instructor explained that people in the provinces lacked the necessary education to grasp engineering fundamentals, the volunteers got their first surprise. They had been told that training young Tanganyikans the fundamentals of engineering was an integral part of their work.

"What about maps?" a volunteer-surveyor asked. "Maps? You make the maps," the instructor said.

Despite these rather rude beginnings, the Peace Corps contingent recovered nicely. For two years this group of Peace Corps civil engineers were in the front rank of all major highway construction in Tanganyika. The engineering problems in the country were, and are today, immense. Tanganyika, a nation the size of France, Belgium, and Germany combined, has fewer than 800 miles of paved roads. Small wonder that a local official described Peace Corps activity in the country as performing a service that he classed as "absolutely vital."

Although situated just below the equator beside the great lakes of Central Africa, Tanganyika boasts rich and fertile plains and high plateaus. With a population of 9,000,000, it is basically an agricultural country and its people need markets for their crops. (Sisal is the most important crop; coffee and cotton are next in importance.) The markets exist, but during the rainy season there are long months when the villages are isolated from the rest of the country. All-weather roads have become an economic must. This situation has served as the basis for much of Peace Corps activity in Tanganyika.

Tanganyika was originally administered as a League of Nations Mandate and later as a United Nations Trusteeship under the United Kingdom. The nation became independent on December 9, 1961, and a year later became a republic with an elected president.

The day-to-day work of the American Peace Corps engineers in the country is seldom without a touch of the unusual. Art Young, a volunteer from Schwenksville, Pennsylvania, recalls that he was occasionally driven from his surveying and mapping chores by curious elephants. And always there were contrasts between the new world and the old. A 70-cent-a-day pick-and-shovel laborer often worked alongside a modern crawler tractor with a hydraulic ripper.

Lee Hedges of Sterling City, Texas, a Peace Corps surveyor, worked near the Kenya frontier, surveying a site for a jet airfield. But he couldn't keep his stakes in the ground. Members of the Masai tribe thought the stakes pointed to buried treasure and dug them up every night. Native stake thieves also frustrated the work of Roger Hagler of Jonesboro, Louisiana; they took his markers for firewood. Roger was able to complete his work only by resorting to a local brand of sorcery. He learned to fend off the tribesmen by tying a tuft of grass around each stake.

Volunteers describe the average Tanganyikan as pro-American. "However, the view is somewhat distorted," said one, "due to the image of America presented by the local movie houses in the capital city, Dar es Salaam, which portray the idea that America is still the land of cowboys and Indians, Chicago gangsters, and adulterous wives."

From the outset, volunteers dismissed the British notion that Africans would not work. On a safari, when their African helper sat down, saying he could not go on, two volunteers, Thomas Katus of McIntosh, South Dakota, and Jerry Parsons of Albany, New York, sat down, too. "Okay," they told their friend. "It's your country; why should we bother?" This got the team moving again.

Jerry, 26, a Negro, was assigned as a surveyor with the first Tanganyika engineering program. He recalls he was an "overnight sensation in the country." When he first arrived in the country, none of the natives would talk to him. Finally, he asked why he was being snubbed. "I found that they thought I was one of the Wachanga tribe, known for its wealth, its superior education, and its snobbery. These people had never seen a black American."

In Nairobi, when the Africans learned that Jerry was an American Negro, he found himself to be a hero. "I seemed to them to be a missing link, and whatever they could do for me was not enough." Jerry says, "I was hailed as 'My Brother,' 'Watanganyika,' and 'Negro Bwana.' The people tried to entice me to stay by offering me a shamba—a wife —and a farm."

Jerry remembers that there were two questions that were asked of him concerning racial conditions in the United States. He was repeatedly asked why Negroes in the United States didn't return home "to help their brothers." And the natives also wanted to know why the United States did not send more Negroes to Africa.

In addition to their prime task of helping to construct a network of farm-to-market roads, the geologists of the project mapped about 7,500 square miles of land for mineral deposits. Surveyors and engineers worked on harbors, water lines, and drainage systems and sites for airports, bridges, and even entire towns. They designed a spillway for a dam that threatened to burst; they helped to construct bridges and culverts.

Adding to the project of surveyors and engineers, the Peace Corps in June, 1962, assigned a group of 22 nurses to Tanganyika. The following year 80 additional volunteers were assigned to the country as teachers in the elementary schools.

John Leydon, a leading British geologist, and a director of and a consultant to several diamond, chemical, and mining companies in Tanganyika, describes the Peace Corps engineers and surveyors as doing a "first class job in the bush on basic mapping. These youngsters are showing Africa what Americans are really like," he said. "These young people are showing that America has something much more valuable to give than money."

Turkey

In Turkey, there are no mud huts, no starving villagers; the population is adept at raising chickens and digging irrigation ditches. Turkey is not one of the under-developed nations of the world. In fact, in the past two decades, the country has made impressive strides economically and socially.

Yet despite this advantage, the Peace Corps program in Turkey, involving some 140 volunteers in teaching and agricultural work, has not functioned with great success. At least it did not work well in the beginning. Volunteers found that assignments in this relatively well-developed country presented their own set of problems. Today's volunteers in Turkey, learning from past errors, operate with a greater degree of efficiency and success than did earlier contingents.

The first problem was simply one of relationship, of communication between officials of the United States and Turkey. In the years following World War II, Turkey and the United States became closely allied, and the two countries have remained friendly since. The word "NATO" is a part of the Turkish language. So is "PX." Yet, the first Peace Corps volunteers found the Turkish government to look upon their group favorably though quite formally. The Turks were reluctant to allow the volunteers into the smaller villages of the nation where the bulk of the work was to be done.

Also, there was little general knowledge of the Peace Corps or what it was meant to do. It was simply considered an extension of one or another of our aid programs.

Then there was the problem of language. Some of the volunteers felt that they had not been properly trained to speak Turkish. To the teaching volunteers, this was a severe problem. They found it to be difficult to maintain classroom discipline and to be less than adequate in their teaching of the English language and grammar.

Turkey is often classed as the geographical link between the East and the West and because of this position, the country has held an important status in world affairs since the 14th century. Until the early 1900's, Turkey, as represented by the Ottoman Empire, was a world power of the

first order. During World War I, the gradual disintegra-
tion of the empire was completed, and two decades passed
before the country, under the dynamic Ataturk, emerged as
a strong, revitalized sovereign state.

Turkey today is still largely an agricultural country,
with 80 per cent of its close to 30 million people drawing a
living from such products as tobacco, cotton, cereals, figs,
and olives.

Istanbul, with a population of over a million people, is
the biggest city; Ankara and Izmir are other large cities, yet
more than 80 per cent of the population lives in one or
another of the more than 40,000 villages scattered about the
country. Generally speaking, the volunteers serve in the
country's "middle-sized" villages, those of 15,000 to 50,000
in population.

The first group of volunteers, a contingent of just 39,
arrived in Turkey in September, 1962. A year later, two
additional projects with a total of about 100 volunteers,
were assigned to the country. Eight of the original volunteers were assigned agricultural tasks, working in soil conservation, irrigation, and forestry. The balance of the
group set to work teaching English in Turkish secondary
schools.

During the first year of the education project, the results
were less than effective. The classes were large—60 to 90
students. And in the Turkish educational system, cheating
on examinations is often an accepted practice. These fac-
tors, combined with the volunteer's lack of training in the
language, made the maintaining of discipline a difficult
classroom task.

After five months of teaching, one volunteer reported,

"I haven't yet got beyond the stage of calling, 'Please sit down,' or, 'Please make less noise.' "

In Turkish schools, volunteers found that maintaining discipline by means of physical force is a normal practice. To slap a student is quite usual. One volunteer, facing a severe discipline problem, attempted the practice—and got a violent slap in return.

Despite the lack of classroom decorum, the Turkish school system itself is a rigid one. Government approved textbooks are a must. Any deviation from the normal course of study is frowned upon. Extra-curricular activities are established only with the greatest of difficulty. An innovation like an English club requires "explanations and justifications that would tax an experienced diplomat," as one volunteer put it.

Despite the frustrations, there have been some accomplishments. Volunteer teachers have been able to organize voluntary English clubs in a dozen different towns, and at least three English language newspapers are being published by students. Two Peace Corps groups have organized lending libraries. A Peace Corps couple from Alexandria, Virginia, has started a "sister town" project; citizens from Alexandria are collecting books for their sister city in Turkey.

From a social standpoint, the volunteers have been gratified over the results of their assignments. Since they live not as tourists nor as government officials, they have been able to gain a keen insight into the community aspects of Turkish life.

The agricultural technicians, at least in the beginning, found greater problems than the teachers. The country's agricultural system, outside of the villages, is well-planned and well-staffed. The Turks pride themselves on a some-what sophisticated knowledge of farm methods. But in the villages, where agricultural techniques are rather primitive, Peace Corps volunteers have not been allowed to work.

Only one of the original group of agricultural workers still holds the job first assigned him in the country. Some volunteers have moved as many as three or four times. They seek assignments where they can work with efficiency and effectiveness.

One volunteer was first assigned to Mersin, a town of 40,000 people in Southern Turkey where the growing sea-son is the longest. He stayed in Mersin four months, "some-times working, sometimes not," he says. From Mersin, he moved to Ankara, and working out of the city, he began a study of agricultural problems of ten villages in an effort to improve farming methods. But though the program went fairly well, authorities inscrutably requested he dis-continue his work. Again he was transferred. Other volun-teers on agricultural assignments report similar frustra-tions.

Volunteers continually find that Turks living outside the large population centers have only a sparse knowledge of the United States. For example, two volunteer teachers were the first Americans ever to reside in Bursa, a city of 150,000 people.

To the Turks, the Peace Corps volunteer represents a "new type" of American. It is a great change for the native population to see Americans who live on $60 a month, do their own cooking and shopping, travel by bus or bicycle, and even speak or attempt to speak the difficult Turkish language. As one volunteer said, "They feel there must be a catch somewhere."

Of course, there is no catch. And demonstrating that there is none to the Turkish citizen may be the greatest contribution the volunteers have made. The Peace Corps program in Turkey—in its first year of operation—was largely one of orientation. As one official expressed it, at its mid-point, the Peace Corps program in Turkey had been a program "of frustration, progress, and hope, and the greatest of these is hope."

Appendix

PEACE CORPS TRAINEES AND VOLUNTEERS
LATIN AMERICA

Country	Number of Projects[1]	Volunteers in Training[2]	Volunteers in Host Country	Total
Bolivia	6	34	122	156
Brazil	7	52	218	270
British Honduras	1	—	29	29
Chile	4	—	108	108
Colombia	15	261	367	628
Costa Rica	2	—	68	68
Dominican Republic	7	61	152	213
Ecuador	7	44	238	282
El Salvador	2	—	48	48
Guatemala	3	68	60	128
Honduras	2	41	28	69
Jamaica	3	37	38	75
Panama	3	—	18	18
Peru	10	35	370	405
St. Lucia	2	—	17	17
Uruguay	1	—	18	18
Venezuela	5	—	103	103

[1] The term "projects" refers to individual contingents of volunteers.

[2] Volunteers "in training" are those undergoing field or classroom study at a United States college or university prior to assignment to the country indicated.

PEACE CORPS TRAINEES AND VOLUNTEERS
AFRICA

Country	Number of Projects	Volunteers in Training	Volunteers in Host Country	Total
Cameroon	3	—	90	90
Ethiopia	2	—	415	415
Gabon	3	27	54	81
Ghana	5	—	140	140
Guinea	2	—	57	57
Ivory Coast	3	—	56	56
Liberia	3	—	285	285
Morocco	2	—	106	106
Niger	2	—	15	15
Nigeria	8	130	382	512
Nyasaland	3	67	44	111
Senegal	3	—	66	66
Sierra Leone	3	—	131	131
Somali Republic	1	—	31	31
Tanganyika	2	—	111	111
Togo	2	—	38	38
Tunisia	3	—	92	92

PEACE CORPS TRAINEES AND VOLUNTEERS
FAR EAST

Country	Number of Projects	Volunteers in Training	Volunteers in Host Country	Total
Indonesia	2	19	17	36
Malaya	5	86	163	249
Sabah/Sarawak	3	61	86	147
Philippines	9	—	591	591
Thailand	7	34	260	294

NEAR EAST AND SOUTH ASIA

Afghanistan	3	39	35	74
Ceylon	1	—	34	34
Cyprus	1	—	22	22
India	5	55	129	184
Iran	2	—	46	46
Nepal	2	—	102	102
Pakistan	7	64	196	260
Turkey	3	—	145	145

PEACE CORPS TRAINEES AND VOLUNTEERS

Area	Number of Projects	Volunteers in Training	Volunteers in Host Countries	Total
Africa	50	224	2113	2337
Far East	26	200	1117	1317
Latin America	80	651	2024	2675
Near East & South Asia	24	158	709	867
TOTAL	180	1233	5952	7196

PEACE CORPS ORGANIZATION PLAN

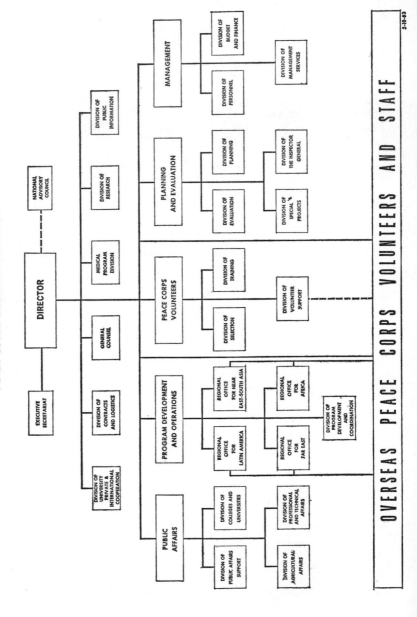

DIRECTOR

NATIONAL ADVISORY COUNCIL

EXECUTIVE SECRETARIAT

DIVISION OF UNIVERSITY PRIVATE & INTERNATIONAL COOPERATION

DIVISION OF CONTRACTS AND LOGISTICS

GENERAL COUNSEL

MEDICAL PROGRAM DIVISION

DIVISION OF RESEARCH

DIVISION OF PUBLIC INFORMATION

PUBLIC AFFAIRS
- DIVISION OF PUBLIC AFFAIRS SUPPORT
- DIVISION OF COLLEGES AND UNIVERSITIES
- DIVISION OF PROFESSIONAL AND TECHNICAL AFFAIRS
- DIVISION OF AGRICULTURAL AFFAIRS

PROGRAM DEVELOPMENT AND OPERATIONS
- REGIONAL OFFICE FOR LATIN AMERICA
- REGIONAL OFFICE FOR NEAR EAST-SOUTH ASIA
- REGIONAL OFFICE FOR FAR EAST
- REGIONAL OFFICE FOR AFRICA
- DIVISION OF PROGRAM DEVELOPMENT AND COORDINATION

PEACE CORPS VOLUNTEERS
- DIVISION OF SELECTION
- DIVISION OF TRAINING
- DIVISION OF VOLUNTEER SUPPORT

PLANNING AND EVALUATION
- DIVISION OF EVALUATION
- DIVISION OF PLANNING
- DIVISION OF SPECIAL PROJECTS
- DIVISION OF THE INSPECTOR GENERAL

MANAGEMENT
- DIVISION OF PERSONNEL
- DIVISION OF BUDGET AND FINANCE
- DIVISION OF MANAGEMENT SERVICES

OVERSEAS PEACE CORPS VOLUNTEERS AND STAFF

5-10-63